Dufton Church

THE OLD
PARISH CHURCHES
OF CUMBRIA

Mike Salter

FOLLY PUBLICATIONS

ACKNOWLEDGEMENTS

The photographs and measured drawings in this book are the product of the author's fieldwork between 1970 and 1998. Old postcards, prints and brass rubbings are reproduced from originals in the author's collection. Thanks are due to Max Barfield, Chris and Frances Bowers, Mike Jackson and Peter Ryder for accommodation. Peter also provided a lot of useful information about various churches.

ABOUT THIS BOOK

As with the other books about churches in this series (see the full list on the inside of the back cover) this book concentrates on the period before the Industrial Revolution of the late 18th century necessitated the construction of a fresh series of churches to serve new urban areas. Most furnishings and monuments after 1790 are not mentioned but additions and alterations to the fabric ususally are, but with less detail. Churches founded after 1790 are mostly not mentioned in the gazetteer, nor do they appear on the map. They are, however listed towards the back of the book.

The book is inevitably very much a catalogue of dates and names, etc. It is intended as a field guide and for reference rather than to be read from cover to cover. Occasionally there is a comment about the setting of a church but on the whole little is said about their position or atmosphere. The amount of material given for a particular church in this book is not necessarily a true indication of how interesting or attractive the building may be. Notable features of a church or its graveyard may lie outside the scope of this book as outlined above. The gazetteer features Ordnance Survey grid references (these are the two letters and six digits which appear after each place-name and dedication) and is intended to be used in conjunction with the O.S. 1:50,000 scale maps. These are vital for finding the more isolated buildings.

Plans redrawn from originals in the author's field notes are reproduced to a common scale of 1:400. The buildings were measured in metres and only metric scales are given. For those who feel a need to convert three metres is roughly equal to ten feet. A system of hatchings common to all the plans is used to denote the different periods of work. On some pages there may be insufficient space for a key to the hatching to be shown. Where this is the case refer to another page. The plans should be treated with care and cross-referenced with the text since there are some things difficult to convey on small scale drawings (e.g. stones of one period being reused in the different period, sometimes in a different location.

ABOUT THE AUTHOR

Mike Salter is 45 and has been a professional author-publisher since he went on the Government Enterprise Allowance Scheme for unemployed people in 1988. He is particularly interested in the planning and layout of medieval buildings and has a huge collection of plans of churches and castles he has measured during tours (mostly by bicycle and motorcycle) of all parts of the British Isles since 1968. Wolverhampton born and bred, Mike now lives in an old cottage beside the Malvern Hills. His other interests include walking, railways, board games, morris dancing, morris dancing, playing percussion instruments and calling dances with a folk group.

ISBN 1 871371 35 6

Copyright 1998 by Mike Salter.
First published December 1998.
Folly Publications, Folly Cottage, 151 West Malvern RD, Malvern, Worcs, WR14 4AY
Printed by Severnside Printers, Bridge House, Upton-on-Severn, Worcs, WR8 0HG

Hawkshead Church

CONTENTS

Inside the front cover is a map of churches in the gazetteer.

Corney Church

INTRODUCTION

Very little Saxon masonry remains in the fabric of the parish churches of Cumbria. Morland has a tower which is perhaps early 11th century, there is a doubtful window at Cumwhitton and evidence of the east end of the nave at Crosby Garrett. However there are other important relics in the form of hogback-shaped tombstones and a fine series of crosses decorated with patterns and figures. Thirty churches have one or other of these, most of them fragments lying either on the floor inside, or outside in the churchyard. Only a few crosses still stand vertical. The Bewcastle cross and its twin at Ruthwell in Dumfriess-shire are superbly carved and as good as anything remaining from their period (late 7th century) in the whole of Europe. The others are later, with a particularly good one of the late 10th century at Gosforth, and others at Burton-in-Kendale, Dearham, and Kirkby Stephen.

Cumbria did not come under the control of the Norman kings of England until 1092 and it reverted to Scottish rule from 1136 to 1157. Little of the work noted as Norman in the gazetteer predates the 1130s. Long Marton and Ormside have remains of mid to late 11th century naves, and a tympanum at St Bees may also be that early. Of greater importance is the massive north arcade of c1110-15 at Kikby Lonsdale which is directly copied from work then just completed at Durham Cathedral. About this time Cumbria became a see with a cathedral at Carlisle. It is just possible that the rare arcaded apse at Warwick is a copy of the original east end of Carlisle Cathedral which was replaced by a spacious new choir in the 13th century.

Saxon cross, Bewcastle

Norman capital, Lowther

Porch at Caldbeck

Cross-shaft at Dearham   *Chancel arch, Kirkbride*

A quarter of the 160 churches described in the gazetteer are essentially buildings of the period 1130-1200.Most have been considerably altered, rebuilt and extended by later centuries but some retain their original modest form with only minor alterations. Most parish churches of this period were small and simple as first built, comprising a nave with a south doorway and one or two small round-headed windows with deep internal embrasures on each side and a round arch opening into a square chancel which contained the altar. Denton chapel is a modest example of this, whilst at Isel and elsewhere each chamber is made rather longer.

Some churches are more ambitious and others soon needed more space for growing congregations. A dozen churches had an aisle built on one side of the nave or under construction by the year 1200, and at Lowther and three other places there were aisles on both sides. These aisles were originally dark narrow passages and have nearly always been altered later on. At the very least bigger windows would be provided, but more often the whole aisle was taken down later and rebuilt wider and sometimes longer as well. Thus the arcades survive more often than the outer walls. The arches are round, normally with a step, and piers and responds are usually circular, or occasionally octagonal. Chamfers on the arches appear later in the 12th century. Appleby, Bolton, Burton-in-Kendal, Dacre, Kirkby Lonsdale, Long Marton and Ormside all have or had west towers of c1130-1200.No transepts earlier than 1200 survive in the stock of purely parochial churches, but what are now parish churches at Abbeytown, Cartmel, Lanercost, and St Bees were monastic churches planned on a rather larger scale, all of them originally cruciform with transepts and central towers. Each of them took so long to build that their construction spans both the 12th and 13th centuries with characteristics of each period in different parts. Carlisle Cathedral was also originally a large cruciform monastic church of c1120-60.

Bridekirk, 12th century

Bowness-on-Solway: 12th century

Dacre: c1200

Wetheral: 16th century

Doorways in Cumbrian Churches

Choir, Cartmel Priory

The pointed arch first appears c1190 but was only universally adopted for all openings a generation later, the style of the decades either side of the year 1200 being known as Transitional. Much of the best work of this period and first half of the 13th century appears in the four monastic churches listed above. Amongst the ordinary parish churches there is much 13th century work but most of it is minor extensions and improvements to older buildings. There is nothing to compare with the fine series of 13th century chancels in Northumberland. Scaleby is an example of a modest village church of this period now shorn of its chancel. Seven churches were given transepts but except at Morland and Warcop these have been later destroyed, rebuilt, or swallowed up by the widening and lengthening of aisles. Eight churches have two aisles of this period, or remains of them, and a similar number had a 13th century aisle one side only of the nave. Just four churches have 13th century towers.

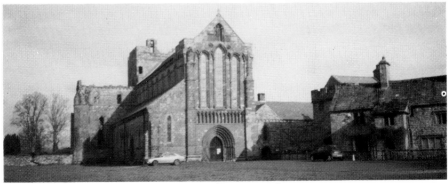

West front of Lanercost Priory

Beetham Church

In other parts of England parish churches have much fine work of the period 1290-1360, but Cumbria has little to show from this era. Much of the church of St Lawrence at Appleby is 14th century, but elsewhere there are only two examples of south transepts and four examples of aisles. Two churches have an aisle with an almond-shaped west window but the fine flowing tracery normal elsewhere for this period is absent. This was the period when the Scots began to raid northern England and the towers at Burgh-by-Sands and Great Salkeld were designed to be defensible. At Newton Arlosh the whole of the small church was defensible. This building resembles, especially in plan-form, a number of late medieval churches in eastern Ireland but has no parallel elsewhere in England, Wales or Scotland.

Aldingham Church

Most of the pre-Reformation stock of churches have some work of the period when the Perpendicular style was in vogue from the late 14th century to the mid 16th century but in Cumbria it is mostly in the form of minor alterations and additions to existing buildings. Large new windows were a common improvement and the widening of aisles sometimes occurred. There are no transepts of this period except at Boltongate, where both they and the nave have have pointed tunnel vaults (more normal in Scotland than England). There are surprisingly few towers, and what chapels there are take the form of eastern extensions to aisles. The most extreme form of this occurs at Kendal, where there the nave and chancel, inner aisles and wide outer aisles extend without interuption to the east end. This is also seen at Crosthwaite and Bowness-on-Windermere which are mostly of this period. There are no complete examples without earlier or later work. What windows remain have quite modest tracery and after 1500 there is an increasing tendency for them to be straight-headed with the lights just round-arched without tracery or cusping.

In Cumbria the Gothic style remained in fashion until the 17th century. There is a complete church begun 1609 at Arthuret which would pass for being a hundred years older but for one or two slight details. Of about the same period is the east window at Abbeytown, whilst Greystoke has a chancel dated 1645. In the 1650s and 60s the Lady Anne Clifford erected single chambers at Brougham and Mallerstang with single light windows either round-headed or pointed. Of the same period are the churches of Soulby and Witherslack. There is much 17th century work in the churches generally but the rest of what survives is minor except for the complete rebuilding of the exterior in Lowther in the 1680s. In and around the mountains there are many dale-chapels dating from any time from the 1540s to the late 18th century. Few can be dated more precisely as all are plain rectangles with low side-walls pierced by simple domestic-looking windows with or without mullions, and often in any case renewed during the 19th century.

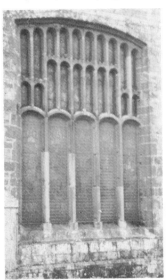

East window, Hulme Cultram

West front, Hulme Cultram (Abbeytown)

Highhead Chapel, now a house

Ulpha Church

Cumbria has over twenty 18th century churches, more than most English counties, partly because new churches were still being founded in the more remote areas. They tend to have wide naves with round-headed or segmental-headed windows and shallow chancels. Most of them have west towers and in the more ambitious churches at Penrith (1720-6) and Whitehaven (1752) the towers contain staircases to upper galleries with their own upper tier of windows. These buildings have classical interiors with Tuscan columns and stucco ceilings. The many 19th century churches resulting from new foundations in industrial areas and total rebuilding of some of the older churches do not concern us here, although they are listed at the back of the book. Almost all of the churches described in the gazetteer were restored some time between 1830 and 1914, many interesting architectural features and furnishings and monuments being swept away in the process.

Uldale Church

Outhgill Church

Threlkeld Church

Font at Ings

Cumbrian churches are not as well furnished as their counterparts further south. In the later medieval period it became the custom for the chancel of a church to be divided off from the nave by a screen with a rood or image of the Crucifixion fixed over it. Sometimes there was a loft over the screen for the use of musicians and the performers of religious plays. Other screens divided off side chapels and transepts. In Cumbria early screens only survive at Greystoke and Kendal and there is little evidence of stairs and upper doorways serving former lofts so perhaps they were uncommon. The other pre-Reformation furnishings comprise five Norman and ten later fonts, stalls with miserichords carved with scenes at Cartmell and Greystoke, fragments of stained glass at a dozen churches, and a door with old ironwork at Heversham. Elizabethan furnishings are rare also, with none of the usual pulpits of that period. From the 17th century rather more remains. There are seven pulpits plus a rare stone one at Brough, a dozen fonts mostly of the 1660s, many communion rails plus benches, pews and panelling. A complete late 17th century interior remains at Brougham. Of the 18th century are many baluster fonts, and again plenty of woodwork such as panelling, pews, communion rails and a few pulpits, including a fine three decker example at Ravenstondale.

Effigies at Crosthwaite

Tomb at Lowther

Tomb at Millom

Brass at Arthuret

Grave slabs at Bridekirk

Coffin-lids with incised or raised crosses are commonly found in Cumbrian parish churches. An accompanying sword indicates a warrior, a chalice for a priest, and shears are thought to be for females. Many are 13th century but the type long remained in use. More ambitious monuments with effigies set in recesses or upon tomb chests are rarer, and most of the two dozen pre-Reformation examples are in the monastic churches of Abbeytown, Carlisle, Cartmel, Lanercost and St Bees. Greystoke and Kendal have collections of early and late 16th century monuments including brasses, of which there are about a dozen in the county, half of them being post-Reformation in date. Of other post-Reformation monuments only three from the 16th century and seven of the 17th century have effigies. Later monuments tend to be mural tablets with long inscriptions, sometimes architectural surrounds, urns, cherubs, symbols of death or of a profession. A dozen 17th century examples and sixteen 18th century examples are noted in the gazetteer entries.

Tomb in choir of Lanercost Priory

GAZETTEER OF CHURCHES

ABBEYTOWN   *St Mary*   NY 178508

The Cistercian abbey of Hulme Cultram was founded by Prince Henry, son of King David of Scotland in 1150. When Henry II of England took over Cumbria he confirmed the grant of lands and a fine new church was then built with an aisled nave of nine bays, a crossing and transepts with east chapels, and a straight ended chancel, i.e the usual Cistercian plan. Much of it is only known from excavations since the present church represents just six bays of the nave now shorn of its aisles. The piers have eight shafts with plain or waterleaf type capitals and the arches are pointed with chamfers, i.e not earlier than c1185-90. The arches are now walled up with two tiers of round-headed windows of c1730-5. There is a very fine west doorway with four orders of columns and many mouldings, one of them being keeled and the outermost having a bobbin motif. The doorway was probably once gabled but the walling above it and the double bellcote are 18th century. In front of the doorway is a porch added by Abbot Robert Chamber in 1507, as confirmed by

inscriptions and shields upon it. A tower later added over the crossing fell in 1600, and the church was further damaged by fire in 1604. The present east window must be of that period. Ruins of the parts further east were removed after being depicted by the Buck brothers in 1727. In the porch are fragments of the tomb of Abbot Chamber, including an effigy showing him enthroned and kneeling figures, plus other fragments and coffin lids. There is also a large fragment of a 15th century figure of the Virgin. There are two 17th century chests and a medieval font.

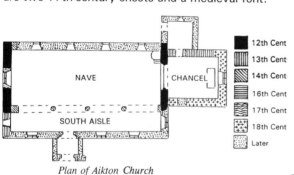

■	12th Cent
▥	13th Cent
▧	14th Cent
▤	16th Cent
▨	17th Cent
▦	18th Cent
░	Later

Arcade in Hulme Cultram Abbey

Plan of Aikton Church

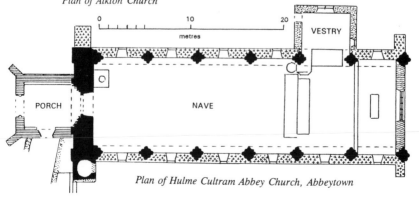

Plan of Hulme Cultram Abbey Church, Abbeytown

Interior of Aldingham Church

AIKTON   *Dedication Unknown*   NY 283529

The narrow Norman chancel arch is single stepped with one order of capitals. The chancel has a 13th century trefoil-headed piscina and the head of a lancet is visible from the vestry but the east and south walls were rebuilt in 1732. The square font with trefoils and the four bay south arcade and south doorway may be 14th century. The narrow aisle was rebuilt in 1869 and the windows are all of about that time.

AINSTABLE   *St Michael*   NY 530468

The church of 1872 by G.Watson has a NW tower and no north windows. It contains a Norman pillar piscina and effigies of John Aglionby, and his wife who died in 1428.

ALDINGHAM   *St Cuthbert*   SD 284711

The chancel of c1300 has three stepped cusped east lancets, a low-side window of two cusped lancets with a transom, a trefoil-headed priest's doorway, and a chancel arch with head-stops. The south arcade of c1190 has round and octagonal piers carrying round arches of two orders, only one of which has a chamfer. The aisle windows are of 1845-6 when a north aisle was also added. The 14th century west tower with has four bold diagonal corner buttresses. One window is 15th century and another, with columns rather than normal mullions, is 17th century. There are box pews inside and a late 17th century communion rail. See page 8.

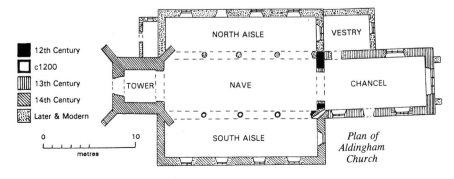

12th Century
c1200
13th Century
14th Century
Later & Modern

NORTH AISLE
VESTRY
TOWER
NAVE
CHANCEL
SOUTH AISLE

0   10
metres

*Plan of
Aldingham
Church*

APPLEBY   *St Lawrence*   NY 684205

The oldest parts are the Norman lower part of the tower with one original north window and the reset 13th century outer entrance of the porch with dogtooth ornament and hollow chamfers. The aisles with irregularly laid out five bay arcades with quatrefoil-shaped piers, the extra bay extending the south aisle alongside the tower, the diagonally buttressed south porch, and the chancel with a two bay arcade to a south chapel are all early 14th century. The east end of the south chapel, the south aisle west window, the chapel screens, the clerestory and the upper part of the tower are 15th century. The Lady Anne Clifford is said to have "caus'd a great part of Appleby Church to be taken down" and rebuilt. Hers are the north chapel of 1654-5 with a two bay arcade and the buttresses at the east end and along the south side. The north buttresses, the bow-ended NW vestry, and most of the windows are 19th century, but rather later than the panelled ceiling of that period.

The organ case has come from Carlisle Cathedral and contains woodwork probably of the 1540s, the 1680s, and the 1830s. The sword-rest is early 18th century. The important monuments are all to females. One is early 14th century with the lower head of the effigy hidden by a foliated cross. The others are to Margaret, Countess of Cumberland, erected 1617, with a recumbent effigy, and to Lady Anne Clifford, Countess of Pembroke, erected before her death in 1676, and without an effigy but having a family tree with twenty-four shields.

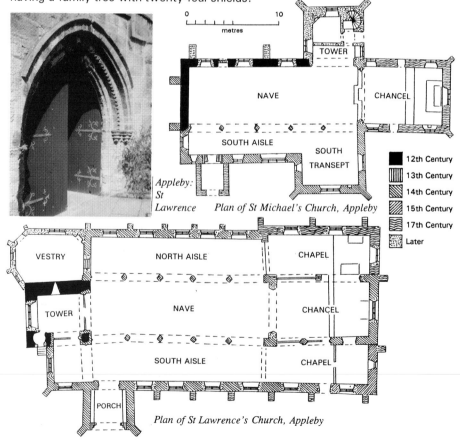

Appleby: St Lawrence

Plan of St Michael's Church, Appleby

0   10
metres

TOWER
NAVE   CHANCEL
SOUTH AISLE
SOUTH TRANSEPT

■ 12th Century
▨ 13th Century
▨ 14th Century
▨ 15th Century
▨ 17th Century
▨ Later

VESTRY   NORTH AISLE   CHAPEL
TOWER   NAVE   CHANCEL
SOUTH AISLE   CHAPEL
PORCH

Plan of St Lawrence's Church, Appleby

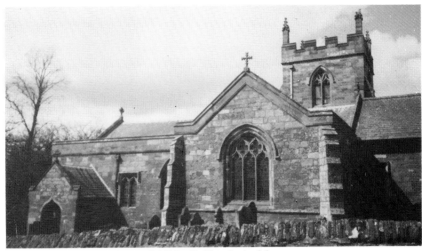

St Michael's Church, Appleby

APPLEBY   *St Michael*   NY 688199

In the chancel is a cartouche with the initials A.P. for the Lady Anne Clifford, Countess of Pembroke. She is said to have rebuilt the church (now privately owned) and the chancel may be her work, although its windows are Victorian. The nave is Early Norman, with a blocked narrow doorway of that period on the north side. The south doorway is 13th century and reset since the aisle and transept with a five bay arcade and the porch are otherwise all early 14th century, except for the ogival-headed porch outer entrance probably of the 1660s. The transeptal north tower is of 1885-6. The arms of the Roos and Vipont families appear on a damaged late 14th century female effigy in a recess on the south side and again on fragments of a tomb canopy reset along with other fragments in the wall of the former vicarage nearby.

St Lawrence's Church, Appleby

ARMATHWAITE   *Christ & Mary*   NY 506462

According to the will of Richard Skelton the small single chamber with rounded-headed side windows with one hollow chamfer was "built before 1668". The east window has two lights under a square head.

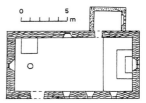

Plan of Armathwaite Church

ARTHURET   *St Michael*   NY 379677

This church serves Longtown 1km to the north. When James I came to the English throne in 1603 it was in a poor state of repair and he allowed money to be collected throughout the kingdom for rebuilding, which began in 1609. The quatrefoil shaped piers inside may be a relic of the older building, perhaps 13th century. The westernmost piers of the five bay arcades and those of the two bay chancel chapels are much smaller and octagonal. Both the aisles and the clerestory are embattled and the windows have four-centered heads to the lights so the building looks two or three generations older than its actual date. It has a fine west tower with diagonal buttresses. The original east window now lies in the garden of Whoof House at Warwick. It has two pairs of three lights under segmental arches with intersecting tracery above and a vertically set oval in the middle of the top, a motif one might normally expect later in the 17th century. The brass plate of c1400 with hands holding a heart in front of a florated cross commemorates a heart burial. There are modest monuments to Sir George Graham, d1657, and Dr Robert Graham, d1782.

Armathwaite Church

ASKHAM   *St Peter*   NY 518238

The church was entirely rebuilt in 1832 to a neo-Norman design by Robert Smirke. The only older relics are a plain font dated 1661, an Elizabethan tomb chest, and some tablets to the the Sandford family of Askham Hall.

Arthuret Church

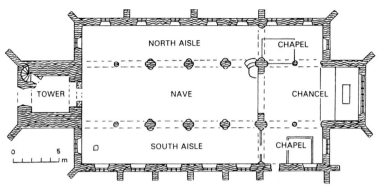

Plan of Arthuret Church

ASPATRIA   *St Kentigern*   NY 147419

The church was entirely rebuilt in 1846-8 by Travis & Mangnall, the style being Early English except for the tower. Inside are a 13th century square font with patterns of leaves, a section of the shaft of an Anglo-Danish cross-shaft with interlace, several other pierces of early crosses, a hogback coffin lid, a monument to Sir Richard Musgrave, d1710, and a Norman arch now forming part of the vestry doorway.

BAMPTON   *St Patrick*   NY 522180

The square font with a round arch on each side may be Norman, despite being dated 1662. The church was rebuilt in 1726-8 and of that period are the west tower with a narrow doorway with a broken segmental pediment, the seven bays of thin arched side windows, the wooden columns, and the pulpit and communion rail. The arches connecting the columns to the outer walls and the nave upper parts are of 1885.

Bampton Church

Barton Church

BARTON *St Michael* NY 487264

All four corners of the Norman nave survive plus the reset north doorway with a continuous roll-moulding. Also Norman is the barrel-vaulted lower stage of a central tower with a small window on the south side and original east and west arches of two orders, the responds being cut away for the insertion of lower strainer arches in the 14th century. A new chancel was then added and the tower heightened. Visible on the tower east side is the roof mark of a smaller Norman chancel. The south aisle with a three bay arcade on octagonal piers is mid or late 13th century, but the round arched south doorway with two orders of shafts can hardly be later than c1200. The north aisle with an arcade of quatrefoil-shaped piers is of c1280-1300. The south chapel and the windows in the nave west wall and north aisle are 16th century. The porch and communion rail and the stables on the tower north side are 17th century.

BASSENTHWAITE *St Bega* NY 227287

The church near the lake has an unmoulded Norman chancel arch and single wide 16th century arches with a slight chamfer towards each of the south chapel and south aisle. The windows are mostly of the 1874 restoration. There are Royal Arms of George II and several 18th century memorials to the Wane family. The church of St John by the main road nearer the village is of 1878 by D.Brade.

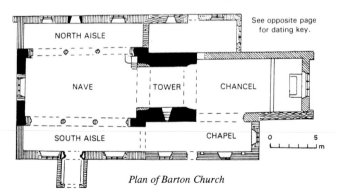

See opposite page for dating key.

NORTH AISLE

NAVE TOWER CHANCEL

SOUTH AISLE CHAPEL

0   5
⊢——————⊣ m

Plan of Barton Church

Tower at Bampton

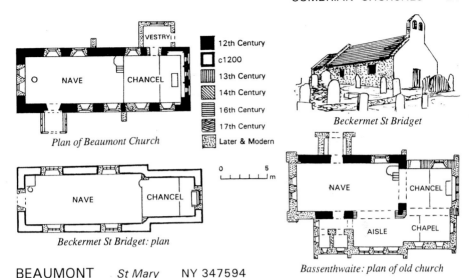

Legend	
■	12th Century
▢	c1200
▥	13th Century
▨	14th Century
▤	16th Century
▩	17th Century
▦	Later & Modern

Plan of Beaumont Church

Beckermet St Bridget

Beckermet St Bridget: plan

0   5
└─┴─┴─┴─┘ m

Bassenthwaite: plan of old church

BEAUMONT   *St Mary*   NY 347594

The single chamber set on a motte is mostly late 12th century but most of the windows, the south porch, the buttresses, and the vestry are 19th century. Original are the south doorway, and the three east windows with arcading inside and out. Internally the arcading returns one bay on the north side. The arrangement looks lopsided now so perhaps there has been rebuilding on the south. A blocked loop there looks 14th century. The king-post roof is 15th century. There are two cross-slabs.

BECKERMET ST BRIDGET   *St Bridget*   NY 015061

The roughcast nave and chancel are of uncertain date. To the south are two cross-shaft fragments, one Saxon and the other inscribed "Edith, little maid" dated c1103.

BECKERMET ST JOHN   *St John*   NY 019067

The church was rebuilt in 1878-9 by J.Birtley. There are several cross-slabs and fragments of Anglo-Danish crosses, including a socket stone and a cross-head.

Interior of Bassenthwaite Old Church

Bewcastle Church

BEETHAM *St Michael* SD 496796

The four bay south arcade with chamfered round arches on circular piers with scallop capitals to the responds is Norman. Also late 12th century is the west tower, curiously placed off-centre to the nave. The corbelled-out bell-stage is 16th century. The three bay north arcade and the two bay arcades to north and south chapels are 15th century, as are many of the windows and the battlements on the south aisle and south chapel. There are stained glass figures of that period in windows in the south chapel and tower. Two damaged 15th century effigies of members of the Beetham family lie on a tomb chest in the south chapel. The font cover is of 1636. Photo p8.

BEWCASTLE *St Cuthbert* NY 566746

The east end of the single chamber is original work of c1200 with clasping pilaster buttresses and triple stepped lancets. The rest is early 19th century with a west tower set against the northern part of the west wall. There are no north windows. The celebrated late 7th century cross shaft has a runic inscription commemorating King Alcfrith, son of Oswi who died in 670. The east side has a vine scroll with beasts and birds. The north side has a vine scroll, then a knot panel, then a chequer pattern, more knotwork and then more vine scroll. The south side has alternate panels of vine scroll with knotwork. The west side has Christ holding a scroll in one hand and blessing with the other, whilst St John the Evangelist is below and St John the Baptist is above. The carvings are of high quality and well preserved. See p4.

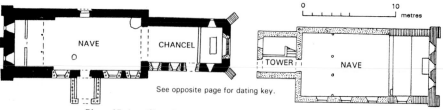

Plan of Bolton Church

See opposite page for dating key.

Plan of Bewcastle Church

Bolton Church

BLAWITH   *St John Baptist*   SD 288882

The existing church is of 1863 by E.G.Paley. Not far to the SW is the featureless ruin of a chapel supposedly built c1560. It looks like a wide "preaching box" of later date.

BOLTON   *All Saints*   NY 639239

The north and south doorways each with one order of columns and the chancel with two original windows are Norman. Another chancel window has been opened out externally into a 13th century lancet. The doorways have saltire crosses on the abaci and have hoodmoulds respectively with a billet and rosettes. The sculptured scene of two knights fighting on horseback over the north doorway is also Norman. The thick-walled west end of the nave with clasping buttresses and two small windows was originally a rectangular tower of which the east wall has been removed and a saddle-back roofed bell-turret added on, probably in the 17th century. The nave south windows and the porch are 18th century. The font cover is of 1687. The effigy of a lady is probably 14th century.

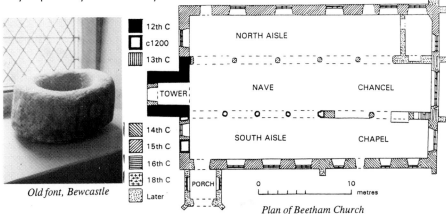

Old font, Bewcastle

Plan of Beetham Church

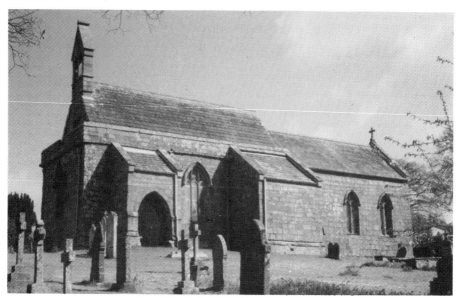

Boltongate Church

BOLTONGATE *All Saints* NY 230408

The whole building appears late 14th century work with windows with two cusped lights with panel tracery. Ralph Neville was the patron. The nave is covered by a steeply pointed stone vault the thrust of which is taken by transepts with half barrel vaults and north and south porches. The corbels at the springing of the vaults perhaps just served to carry the shuttering needed for their construction. Two more corbels inside the west wall carry the bellcote projecting eastwards from the gable, allowing a wall-walk between it and the parapet to the west. The chancel has an original north vestry. The octagonal font is set upon four primitive heads.

BOOT *St Catherine* NY 176012

This is a low single chamber with a 14th century east window, the pointed arch of which has been removed, probably during a 17th century remodelling. The octagonal font with four rosettes and four flowing tracery patterns may be late 17th century. The south porch, the vestry, and the three-light side windows are Victorian.

Boot Church

BOOTLE *St Michael* SD 108884

The transepts are of 1837, and the west tower is of the 1860s or 70s. The nave masonry is Norman with traces of two doorways. The initials on the font may refer to Robert Brown, rector here in the 1530s. A brass depicts Hugh Ashew, d1562.

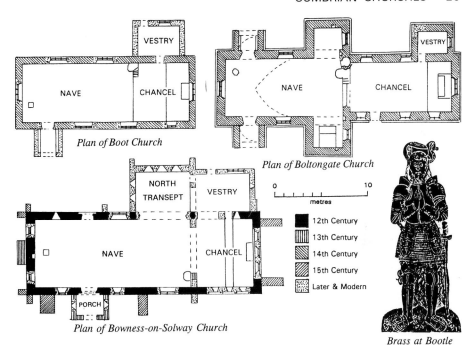

Plan of Boot Church

Plan of Boltongate Church

■	12th Century
▦	13th Century
▨	14th Century
▧	15th Century
▥	Later & Modern

Plan of Bowness-on-Solway Church

Brass at Bootle

BOWNESS-ON-SOLWAY   *St Michael*   NY 224628

The wide single chamber is essentially a Norman building erected with Roman stones from Hadrian's Wall, although most of the windows are of 1891, the probable date of the north transept and vestry and the inserted chancel arch. Original are two north windows, the north and south doorways each with one order of columns, traces of former east windows, and a square font with leaves and a trellis of beaded strips. The north doorway has a continuous roll up the jambs and round the finely moulded arch. The double bellcote with an oblong pyramid roof raised upon a central west buttress and the porch may both be 13th century. The other buttresses are later.

Bowness-on-Solway Church

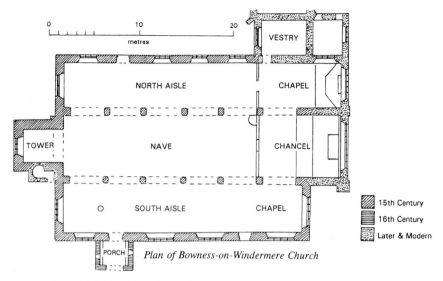

Plan of Bowness-on-Windermere Church

BOWNESS-ON-WINDERMERE   *St Martin*   SD 402969

The tower top with a saddleback roof, the east end and the sprawling NE vestries are of the restoration of 1870 and later, and the clerestory is perhaps 16th century. The rest is probably of the twenty years or so leading up to the consecration recorded in 1483. The aisles are fairly wide and have six bay arcades with plain pointed arches on chamfered square piers. The north windows are of three lights and the much bigger south windows are of four lights with square heads and hood-moulds. The tiny heads on four corners of the octagonal font look Norman. The 15th stained glass in the east window has probably come from Cartmel Priory. The sculpture of St Martin and the Beggar may be 17th century but looks recut.

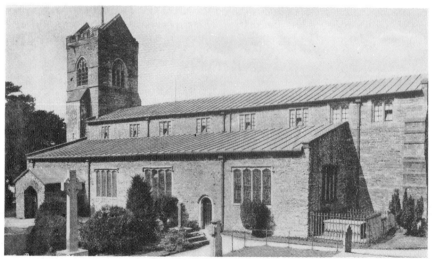

Bowness on Windermere Church

Brampton Old Church

BRAMPTON   *St Martin*   NY 510616

The church in the town is of 1874-8 by Philip Webb. The old church 1.7km to the west comprises a square Norman chancel later lengthened eastwards. Original are one south window and the blocked south doorway. The chancel arch now facing a large porch built on the site of the nave was rebuilt in 1891, the east wall was rebuilt in 1861, and the west corners of the chancel were rebuilt in 1788.

BRIDEKIRK   *St Bride*   NY 117337

Only the chancel with 16th century east and south windows remains in situ of the old church. The cruciform new church of 1868-70 by Cory & Ferguson lies to the west. It has a brick-faced interior and incorporates a Norman doorway with one order of columns with scallop capitals, chevrons at right-angles to the wall and billet hood mounds. The Norman chancel arch is reset over the organ and a 15th century window is reset below the vestry. Several cross-slabs lie against the apse. There is a very fine mid 12th century oblong font carved with affronted dragons, birds, a centaur, a woman with a sword, a man and a woman kneeling by a tree, and a Baptism of Christ. There is also an inscription relating to the sculptor Rikart, who appears in one scene.

Brampton Old Church: plan

0 ... 5 m

■ 12th Cent
▓ 13th Cent
▤ 16th Cent
▒ Later

Plan of Old Chancel, Bridekirk

Chancel of old church, Bridekirk

Brigham Church

BRIGHAM   *St Bridget*   NY 086309

The south arcade of three arches on round piers with square abaci and waterleaf capitals is of c1180-90. The blocked doorway with a small window above it may also be of that date, and the tunnel-vaulted west tower is perhaps of c1200-25, with round abaci on the responds of the tower arch. The twin lancet bell openings are original but the west window is 14th century. The south doorway has a 13th century arch reused when the south aisle was rebuilt in the 14th century. This aisle contained the chantry of St Mary founded by rector Thomas de Bugh in 1323. The west window is almond-shaped with a sunk-quadrant moulding and a slight ogival tip. Thomas's effigy probably once lay in the recess with openwork mouchette tracery and a gable with buttress-like shafts and foliage. The east window has niches for images on either side of it. This window and those on the south were restored by Butterfield in 1864-76. He also added the saddle-back roof of the tower. About that time traces of a Norman apse were discovered. The chancel has one 15th century window and there is another reset in the vestry. The small octagonal font is probably 17th century. The socket remains, with beast heads, of an Anglo-Danish cross-shaft.

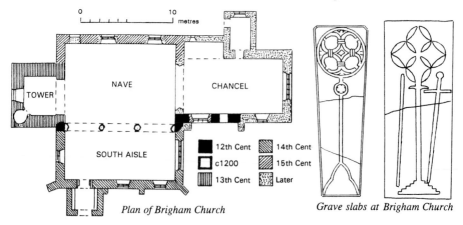

Plan of Brigham Church   *Grave slabs at Brigham Church*

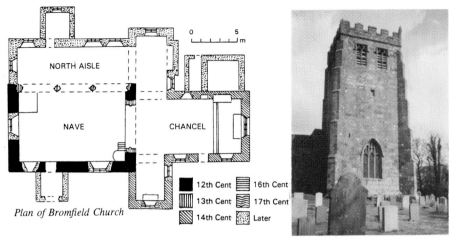

Plan of Bromfield Church

Tower of Brough Church

BROMFIELD *St Mungo* NY 176471

The south doorway has a reset Norman arch with chevrons and sections of a Norman frieze of saltire crosses remain on either side of the later chancel arch with filletted responds. The round piers of the early 13th century north arcade of three bays of round arches also have four fillets. A transept projects southwards from the chancel and has an end window probably of 1687, the date of the sundial. The north transept has been rebuilt along with the aisle and most of the windows in 1860, but the transept east wall still has a recess with a large coffin lid with a recut inscription referring to Adam of Crookdale with the date 1514. Another tomb recess in the north side of the 14th century eastern bay of the chancel contains a tomb chest with an inscription of Roman capitals referring to Richard Garth, d1673. In a field north of the church is a round building containing the holy well of St Mungo.

Bromfield Church

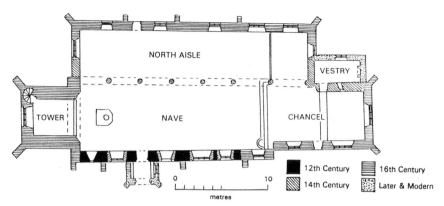

Plan of Brough Church

BROUGH   *St Michael*   NY 794139

The south side of the long nave is Norman, with one original window and a doorway with one order of columns with lozenges on the abaci and human beakhead faces and chevrons on the arches. The six bay arcade and three south windows, and perhaps the recess in the south wall, are 14th century. The west tower is of 1513 and the wide north aisle may be of about the same period, although the stained glass in one window looks 15th century. The chancel may be still later and the east window could be late 17th century like the communion rail. There are plain parapets and the tower and chancel have diagonal buttresses. The plain stone pulpit is of 1624.

Brough Church

St Wilfred's Chapel, Brougham

BROUGHAM *St Ninian* NY 559300

In 1660 the Lady Anne Clifford rebuilt this isolated church by the River Eamont as a single chamber with round-headed single light windows with hoodmoulds between buttresses. There are diagonal corner buttresses, two windows in each of the east and west walls, and two south doorways, that to the west now having a porch of 1841. The roof has collar-beams on long arched braces. A wreath at the east end has the year 1660 and the initials A.P. (Lady Anne was Countess of Pembroke). Of the same period are the font, the screen, the family pews, the benches, the pulpit, a poor-box dated 1666 and the communion rail with dumb-bell shaped balusters.

BROUGHAM *St Wilfred* NY 527284

The chapel of St Wilfred lies beside ruined Brougham Hall. It was rebuilt by the Lady Anne Clifford in 1658 to a similar design as was adopted for the parish church two years later except that there are buttresses set back from the corners instead of diagonally projecting from them and that the window lights are pointed. The font is original. In the 1840 Lord Brougham and Vaux remodelled the interior and brought in much 16th and 17th century woodwork from elsewhere including the screen, stalls panelling and parts of a Flemish triptych and a South German altarpiece.

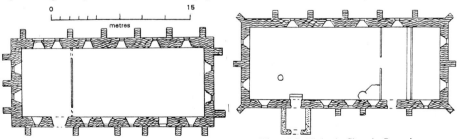

Plan of St Wilfred's Chapel, Brougham   *Plan of St Ninian's Church, Brougham*

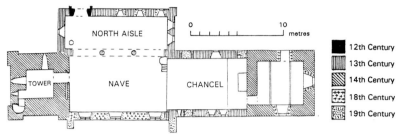

Plan of Burgh-by-Sands Church

BROUGHTON-IN-FURNESS   *St Mary Magdalene*   SD 209875

The Late Norman south doorway has waterleaf capitals on the columns. The east window may be 15th century. The priest's doorway could be early 16th century, and a consecration is recorded in 1547. A wide new neo-Norman nave and chancel in one were added to the north side in 1874 and the tower west of the original nave was added in 1900. The octagonal goblet-shaped font with shields is late medieval.

BURGH-BY-SANDS   *St Michael*   NY 329591

The chancel and north aisle both have restored 13th century lancets and there is a three bay arcade with stiff-leaf capitals on restored octagonal piers. The reset north doorway with beakheads is Late Norman. The mid 14th century tower was defensible, being entered only by a narrow doorway fitted with a drawbar slot and an iron gate or yett. It has thick walls and clasping pilaster buttresses on the western corners. The vestry in an unusual position east of the chancel may have formed a second defensible tower added perhaps c1380-1400. The windows of this part and the top stage of the other tower are 18th century. A south aisle seems to have vanished about that time. There is a large tablet of 1783 on the outside wall.

Norman doorway, Burgh-by-Sands

Tower, Burgh-by-Sands

Burton-in-Kendal Church

BURTON-IN-KENDAL *St James*   SD 530770

The lower part of the broad west tower is Norman with a plain arch towards the nave. The narrow north aisle, the wider south aisle and chapel and the chancel are all 14th century with several original windows. A window of c1300 with cusped intersecting tracery is reset in the east wall of the Victorian vestry. Also Victorian are the chancel buttresses, east window and two bay arcade towards the south chapel. Of the 15th and 16th centuries are the three bay arcades and the north chapel. The Jacobean pulpit has blank arches and other patterns. There are fragments of a Saxon cross-shaft with interlace, chevrons, Christ and other figures, and a wheel-head.

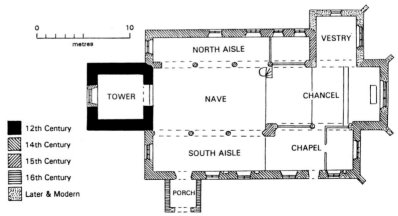

Plan of Burton-in-Kendal Church

Interior of Caldbeck Church

CALDBECK   *St Kentigern*   NY 326399

Much of the church appears early to mid 13th century, with a continuously moulded south doorway and arcades of six bays showing evidence that the western part was built first and then probably the scheme lengthened eastwards. However the discovery of a pier of c1200 in the chancel south wall complicates things, unless it was reused later. The arcade piers are octagonal on the south side and round on the north. The outer entrance of the vaulted 16th century porch is a reused Norman piece with beakheads on either side, suggesting it once formed a narrow chancel arch. Norman masonry may survive in the western part of the chancel north wall. The west tower has a small arch towards the nave and round headed windows. It seems to be of 1727, although a 12th century date has also been claimed for it. Alterations were made by Rector John de Wychdale in 1512. An inscription above it shows that the east window is his and the font may be of that period.

CAMERTON   *St Peter*   NY 036300

The church has a delightful location alone within a bend of the River Derwent. It has a whitewashed nave, chancel and south transept, all 14th century but with features of 1855 when a small west tower with a polygonal top was added. The north side of the chancel was later partitioned off to form a vestry. The effigy of an early 16th century knight is Black Tom Curwen, who was buried at Shap Abbey.

Camerton Church

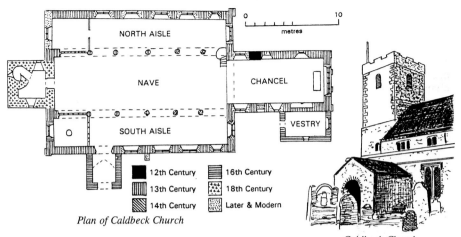

Plan of Caldbeck Church

Caldbeck Church

CARLISLE   *St Cuthbert*   NY 399559

The church lies in a close hidden away from the main open spaces of the city. One north window contains 14th and 15th century stained glass. The church itself is of 1778 and has a west tower, a nave eight bays long with two tiers of windows and galleries on Tuscan columns, and a chancel with a Venetian east window. The nave has doorways at each end. No monuments predate the early 19th century.

In 1988 excavations at 66-69 Scotch Street revealed traces of the chantry chapel of St Alban first mentioned in 1201 and dissolved in 1549. It is thought that at the time of the siege by Robert Bruce in 1315 a church of Holy Trinity stood west of of Caldew Bridge. The church of St Mary built in 1870 and demolished in 1954 had woodwork of the 1760s and a late 15th century door. For other churches see p101.

St Cuthbert's Church, Carlisle

CARTMEL   *St Mary and St Michael*   SD 380788

William Marshal, Earl of Pembroke, founded a priory of Augustinian canons at Cartmel in 1188. The church also served a parish so it was allowed to remain complete after the priory was dissolved in the 1530s, although the other buildings were destroyed apart from the precinct gatehouse. Of the period c1190-1220 are the three bay chancel with two bay arcades of round arches to north and south chapels, the crossing and transepts, and the fine doorway at the SE corner of the nave with three orders of shafts, now opening onto a 17th century porch. The cloister was originally going to be on the south side, hence the position of this doorway and also the doorway in the south transept intended to give access from the dormitory on the upper storey of an intended east range. The cloister and its buildings were eventually erected on the north, necessitating making a new doorway from the dormitory through the north transept north wall, cutting through a lancet window in the process. Work on completing the nave only continued somewhat later in the 13th century, the NE doorway being of that period. Although probably intended to be of six narrower bays the nave as it now stands has only three wide bays, making it rather short for a monastic church. The arcades on octagonal piers and the west front with a five light window for the nave and three light windows in the aisles are all 15th century, as is the top stage of the tower set diagonally, i.e. at 45 degrees to the lower stage, unmoulded arches being provided inside to support this.

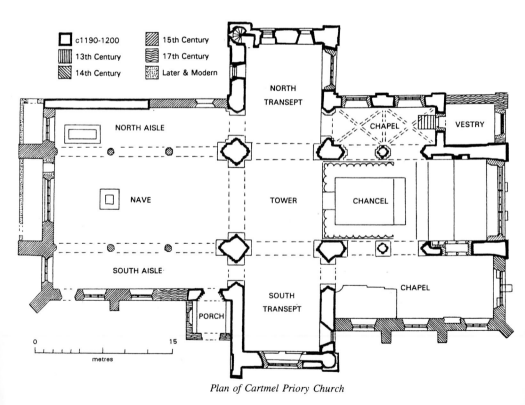

Plan of Cartmel Priory Church

South chapel at Cartmel Priory

The chancel and transepts have flat clasping pilaster corner buttresses typical of their period. The original north chapel of c1200 survives with two bays of quadripartite vaults. There are finely moulded round arches between the chancel and the chapels. The arches have chevrons and lozenges, a motif repeated on the arch from the north transept to the north chapel. This arch, and that towards the north aisle, are, hovever, sharply pointed. The north chapel windows are 15th century and a doorway in the east wall now opens into a 17th century vestry. The chancel has a mutilated set of sedilia and a 15th century nine-light east window. Above the chapel arches are a triforium in the form of a continuous row of pointed arches, and a clerestory which was altered in the 17th century which the present roof was provided. The north transept has a 15th century east window of four lights but the jambs of the embrasure are relics of a pair of original lancets.

The south chapel was replaced c1340 by a wider new chapel of three bays with sedilia with nodding ogival arches. The work was paid for by Lord Harrington, d1347, whose superb tomb chest with effigy and mourners lies under a two bay canopy now set in an arch between the chapel and the chancel. On the canopy posts are shields, square fleurons and figures including Christ and the Virgin. The canopy has carvings of Christ showing his wounds and the Coronation of the Virgin. It hides a wooden ceiling of boards painted with medallions, the signs of the Evangelists, and the feet of a large seated Christ. These look earlier than the 1340s and may be reset from elsewhere. There are tablets with medallions, putti, and urns to Sir William Lowther, d1705 and his wife Katherine, d1700, and Sir Thomas Lowther, d1745, two of them placed against the five light chapel east window in such a way as to block the two outermost lights, giving the window a peculiar shape. Also in the chapel is an effigy of a 13th century Augustinian canon. In a 14th century arch in the chancel north wall is a cross-slab and a Lombardic inscription to Prior William de Walton, d1292.

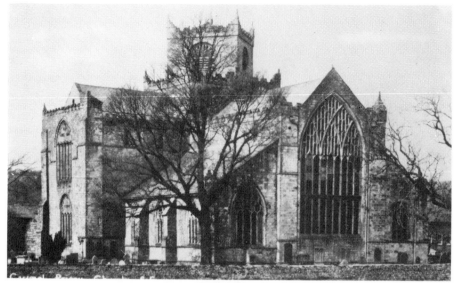

Cartmel Priory

On the nave west wall is a painting of 1646 commemorating the Preston family, especially George Preston. He re-roofed the chancel in 1618-23 and donated the screen and the fine stall backs with columns with trailing vines. The stalls themselves are medieval, bearing the initials of a prior William, either the one elected in 1418, or another elected in 1441. The stalls have miserichords with many interesting scenes carved upon them. On the north appear a unicorn, a green man, a griffin, a face, hounds, an elephant and castle, and on the south appear the signum triciput, a Pelican in her piety, an angel with a shield, a ape with a flask, a mermaid, Alexander carried into the sky by eagles, a dragon, a peacock, and birds. George Preston may also have donated the font cover dated 1640. There is a two tier chandelier of 1734. Parts of a mid 14th century Jesse window remain in the south chapel and some 15th century stained glass figures in the chancel east window.

Cartmel Fell Church

CARTMEL FELL *St Anthony* SD 417881

In 1561 Anthony Knipe made a deposition claiming that the church was built by his father and others fifty-five years earlier. i.e c1505. It has a single main chamber with arched lights without cusps, eastern transepts so shallow as to be little more than recesses, and an unfinished west tower with a saddle-back roof of low pitch. The Cowmire Pew is 16th century and the Burblethwaite Pew is 17th century, although the latter was mostly renewed in 1810. Of 1696 is a pew made up of older bench ends and the three decker pulpit. The east window and one on the north contain 15th century stained glass from Cartmel Priory. The torso of a wooden figure of Christ crucified may be from the same source. It is perhaps as old as the 13th century.

CASTLE SOWERBY *St Kentigern* NY 380362

The nave, the chancel with small lancets (jambs of two more also remain in the east wall), and the reset roll-moulded south doorway are all of c1200-20. The five bay arcade is not much later, but the aisle outer wall and porch are 14th century and the octagonal piers, and the aisle and nave windows, and double bellcote are 16th or 17th century.

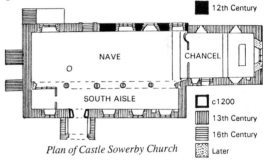

Plan of Castle Sowerby Church

12th Century
c1200
13th Century
16th Century
Later

0   10 metres

CLEATOR *St Leonard* NY 014135

The chancel has one Norman window and there is a 15th century window on the south side. The octagonal font with rolls up the angles is probably of the 1660s. Most of the church dates from the rebuilding of 1841, and the north side with a new entrance and vestries was added in 1900-4 to a design by J.H.Martindale.

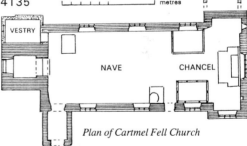

Plan of Cartmel Fell Church

Castle Sowerby Church

Clifton Church

CLIBURN   *St Cuthbert*   NY 587245

The small nave and the chancel with one original window are both Norman but the arch between them is renewed. The east window is a 13th century lancet. Most of the windows are of 1886-7 when a south aisle was added with a two bay arcade to the nave and one towards the chancel. The Norman south doorway was then reset in the aisle wall. The font with shallow chevrons is also Norman.

CLIFTON   *Dedication Unknown*   NY 054291

The small church is entirely of 1858 except for the Norman south doorway with a chamfered arch and a hoodmould with billets and triangles.

CLIFTON   *St Cuthbert*   NY 532271

The Norman nave has a south doorway with a plain tympanum. The porch and one south window may be 16th century and the short north aisle with just one arch towards the nave is perhaps 17th century. In 1846 the nave was given a new west window and the 13th century chancel remodelled and perhaps lengthened. The work included new east lancets, one of which contains 15th century stained glass of the Virgin and St John, and a screen of two columns and three arches instead of a normal chancel arch. The pulpit is made up of old parts.

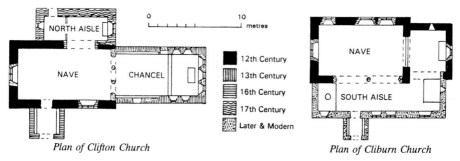

0   10
metres

■ 12th Century
▦ 13th Century
▤ 16th Century
▧ 17th Century
▨ Later & Modern

Plan of Clifton Church   *Plan of Cliburn Church*

COLTON   *Holy Trinity*   SD 318861

A new church consecrated here in 1578 was enlarged in 1721 and 1762. The roughcasted single chamber with a west tower and a north transept now looks Victorian, but the straight-headed windows may be reproductions of late 16th century originals and the priest's doorway and chancel north window look old. The communion rail is 17th century work.

CORNEY   *St John Baptist*   NY 113913

The features are mostly of the restoration of 1882 but some old work survives, such as the west doorway of the nave and the north doorway of the chancel.

CROOK   *St Catherine*   SD 450946

Only the small west tower of c1620 with typical bell-openings and parapet of that period still remains of the old church isolated out in the fields. The new church 0.5km to the north by the main road is of 1887 by Stephen Shaw.

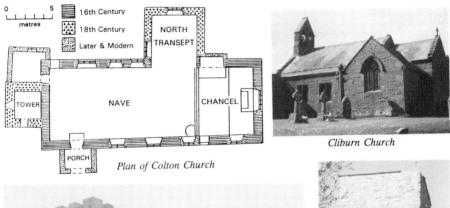

Cliburn Church

Plan of Colton Church

Colton Church

Old Church tower, Crook

CROSBY GARRETT   *St Andrew*   NY 730098

There is evidence of a Saxon opening above the east side of the chancel arch. An aisle added c1175 was rebuilt in 1866 but the three bay arcade of round single-stepped arches on circular piers with flat capitals and leafy abaci still remains. The bell-turret perched on a central west buttress is probably 13th century. The chancel has one 13th century lancet on the north but is otherwise 14th century. The nave south wall may also be a rebuild of that period although the south doorway goes with the porch, which has a beam dated 1662. The window east of the porch and the communion rail are also of that period.

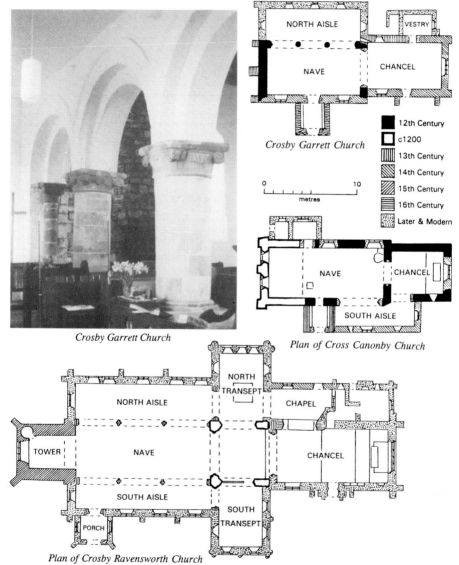

Crosby Garrett Church

Crosby Garrett Church

Plan of Cross Canonby Church

Plan of Crosby Ravensworth Church

12th Century
c1200
13th Century
14th Century
15th Century
16th Century
Later & Modern

0   10
metres

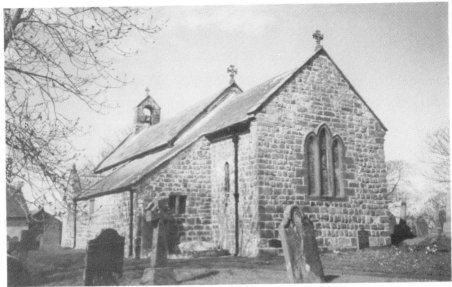

Cross Canonby Church

CROSBY RAVENSWORTH *St Lawrence* NY 622148

The west tower with a higher NW stair turret is late 15th century. Originally, however, a central tower existed or was intended, for the crossing is of 1190-1200 with tripartitite reponds for each triple-chamfered arch. The original chancel arch now lies between the north aisle and the south transept. Of the 13th century are the arch between the south aisle and transept, the arcades of three wide double-chamfered arches on quatrefoil-shaped piers, and the fine south doorway with two orders of columns and a proliferation of dogtooth. The north chapel is 14th century but the wide arch between it and the chancel containing a tomb chest is mid 16th century. The south porch dated 1812 is the work of Robert Smirke, who also provided the elaborate priest's doorway. In the 1850s J.S. Crowther rebuilt the transepts and the aisle outer walls, and in 1875 he rebuilt the chancel, adding a NE vestry.

Crosby Ravensworth

CROSS CANONBY *St John Evangelist* NY 069390

The nave and chancel are both Norman and the arch between them is perhaps Roman work reset. Original are the chancel south window, a south window now visible above an arch (with heads on the responds) to the 14th century south chapel, the doorway with a blank tympanum, and the west buttresses. There is a square 13th century font on five supports with leaf motifs on each side. There are panels of 1730 carved with foliage patterns on the organ gallery and two of the benches. A section of a 10th century cross-shaft shows two dragons biting themselves. Two sides also have interlace. There is also a Saxon or Early Norman coffin lid carved with a cross, chevrons and a man, and an Anglo-Danish hog-back tombstone lies outside.

Crosthwaite Church

CROSTHWAITE   *St Kentigern*   NY 258244

The oldest features are the chancel east wall and buttresses, perhaps 13th century, and the 14th century windows in the north chapel and the shaft of a font donated in the 1390s decorated with traceried windows. The font bowl with leaves and the Sign of the Trinity goes with the rest of the church which is early to mid 16th century. Many straight-headed windows are of that period, and the seven bay arcades not interupted by a chancel arch. The tower is known to date from the 1530s and 40s. One north window has half of a 15th century stained glass figure so some work in the aisle may be of that period, from which also remain effigies of a civilian and wife. On a tomb chest are brasses of Sir John Ratcliffe, d1527, and his wife, patrons for much of the building work. There are many 19th century tablets. See p12.

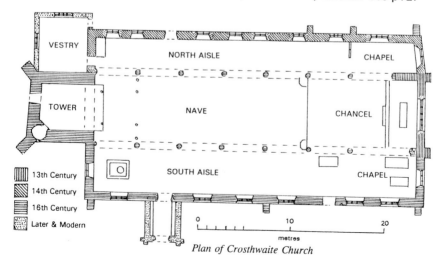

Plan of Crosthwaite Church

CULGAITH   *All Saints*   NY 611298

The cruciform church was consecrated in 1758 and has openings to the transepts with columns rising straight up to the coving of the ceilings. The windows and west porch are Victorian but the panelling is original.

CUMREW   *St Mary*   NY 551503

The rock-faced church with a NW tower is entirely of 1890 by George Dale Oliver. Stones from the 12th century doorway are reset in the 17th century former vicarage by the churchyard entrance. In the churchyard is a defaced early 14th century female effigy with a puppy by her pillow, a cross-shaft and a medieval grave slab.

CUMWHITTON   *St Mary*   NY 506522

The south wall has a Norman fragment with chevrons. The north arcade of three bays with circular piers is of c1200. The aisle outer wall is 18th century and the aisle east window is either of that period or c1200, although it has been claimed to be Saxon. The chancel is 13th century but much rebuilt and there is a thin 19th century west tower with a round arched doorway. The octagonal font is dated 1662.

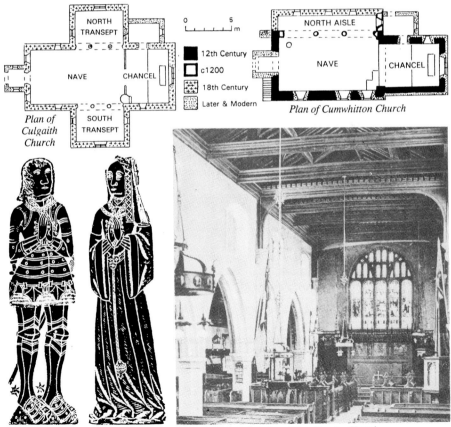

Plan of Culgaith Church

■ 12th Century
□ c1200
18th Century
Later & Modern

Plan of Cumwhitton Church

Brasses at Crosthwaite Church

Interior of Crosthwaite Church

Dacre Church

DACRE   *St Andrew*   NY 460266

The four bears marking the corners of the original churchyard may have come from the castle gatehouse. On two of them are lynxes. The Norman west tower was rebuilt in 1810 except for the plain arch towards the nave. The Late Norman chancel has long round-arched lancets and a doorway with shafts having waterleaf and crocket capitals. The east windows are restored. The north arcade with slight chamfers on the arches and circular piers is of c1200-20 and the south arcade with fuller chamfers and octagonal piers is slightly later. The aisle outer walls are late medieval. The south doorway has a lock dated 1671 with initials of Lady Anne Clifford, Countess of Pembroke. The communion rail is of about the same period. A 9th century cross-shaft fragment has trails and an animal with a human face, and there is also a 10th century cross-shaft with animals, two figures holding hands and Adam and Eve with a tree. The effigy of a cross-legged knight is probably one of the 14th century Dacres.   Other monuments include a cartouche of 1708 to one of the several Edward Hasells. In the north aisle is a chained bible of 1617. Traces of a pre-Norman monastery have been found in excavations north of the church. See page 6.

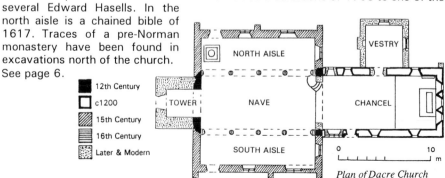

12th Century
c1200
15th Century
16th Century
Later & Modern

VESTRY

NORTH AISLE

TOWER   NAVE   CHANCEL

SOUTH AISLE

0   10
                      m

Plan of Dacre Church

DALSTON   *St Michael*   NY 369502

The early 13th century chancel has a gabled priest's doorway and lancet windows with round rere-arches, there being three of them with stepped heads in the east wall. The aisled nave with timber arcades is mostly of 1749 but the west wall is medieval, the lower part of a Norman doorway remains on the south side and in the porch is a Norman capital with decorated scallops above flowers and leaves.

Dalston Church

DALTON-IN-FURNESS   *St Mary*   SD 226738

The present church is of 1882-5 by Austin & Paley. Of the old church the only relics are fragments of 15th century glass in the north porch.

DEAN   *St Oswald*   NY 071254

The drum-shaped font with intersecting arches is Norman and the nave west and north walls must also be of that period. The south aisle added c1200-20 has a four bay arcade of double-chamfered arches upon circular piers. The tomb recess in the aisle wall and the south porch are a little later. The 13th century chancel was rebuilt in the 15th century and then in the 17th century extended to join up with another building, part of which now forms the east wall. This explains blocked doorways flanking the east window. The vestry and the nave north and west windows are Victorian. The double bellcote on the nave east gable is probably 17th century.

DEARHAM   *St Mungo*   NY 073364

The chancel has Norman windows on either side and the nave has a Norman south doorway with one order of columns with waterleaf on one capital and a deeply moulded arch. The tunnel-vaulted west tower is 14th century. The bell-openings of twin ogival-headed lights must be later, and until the north aisle was added by Ferguson in 1882 there was a doorway instead of an arch towards the nave. The font is a Norman block capital with spirals, volutes, dragons and friezes of arched panels, lozenges and rectangles. There are many medieval coffin lids and fragments of three Anglo-Danish crosses. One has a wheel-head and interlace. Another, called the Kenneth Cross, has a man on a horse, a bird facing a man and scrolls and plaits. A third has a runic inscription below which are rosettes, three figures under arches, a quatrefoil, a bearded head upside down in a semi-circle, and the word Adam.

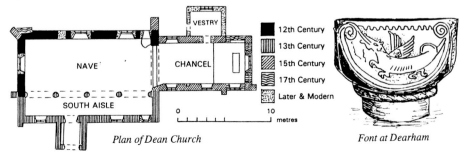

Plan of Dean Church   *Font at Dearham*

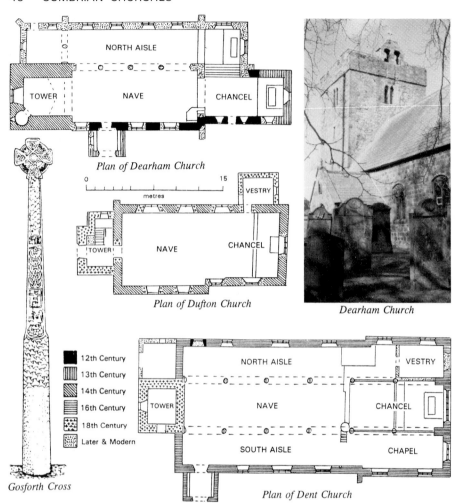

NORTH AISLE

TOWER   NAVE   CHANCEL

Plan of Dearham Church

0   15

metres

VESTRY

TOWER   NAVE   CHANCEL

Plan of Dufton Church

Dearham Church

■ 12th Century

▥ 13th Century

▨ 14th Century

▤ 16th Century

▦ 18th Century

▨ Later & Modern

NORTH AISLE   VESTRY

TOWER   NAVE   CHANCEL

SOUTH AISLE   CHAPEL

Gosforth Cross

Plan of Dent Church

DENDRON   *St Matthew*   SD 246706

An inscription inside the nave west wall records building of a church here in 1642 by a Londoner born in the village. The existing building with five bays of arched windows is of 1795 with a west tower added in 1833.

NAVE   CHANCEL

Plan of Upper Denton Chapel

DENT   *St Andrew*   SD 705871

Much of the church, which is fully aisled with six bay arcades and a five-light east window, is early 16th century. The eastern two bays of the chancel chapels are very slightly wider than the rest. Older parts are the 13th century three western bays of the arcades with double-chamfered arches on circular piers and the blocked Norman north doorway with a plain chamfer. The tower is said to be of 1785. The pulpit is dated 1614 and there are pews dated 1619 and 1693. They have knobs on the ends.

Dent Church

DENTON   *St Cuthbert*   NY 615655

The small nave and chancel church now in private ownership at Upper Denton is Norman work of Roman stones from nearby Hadrian's Wall. Original are the chancel arch, two nave windows and two plain doorways, that on the north being blocked. One window on each side are Victorian. The chancel has two 13th century lancets, one restored. The church of 1868-70 by Cory & Ferguson at Nether Denton 2km SW lies on the site of a Roman fort and contains a small but fine Norman sculpture of a king with a sceptre set against a cross extending beyond a central circle.

DISTINGTON   *Holy Spirit*   NY 006235

The only relic of the old church is the 13th century chancel arch in the churchyard. The new church with a short SE tower is of 1886 by Hay & Henderson.

DUFTON   *St Cuthbert*   NY 685262

The west tower, the windows with Y-tracery, and the canted ceiling with stucco panelling are of 1784 but older masonry survives. It appears that what is now one chamber was originally divided into a nave with a north aisle and a chancel with a vestry. On the south wall is a damaged panel showing a figure in a sunk field.

Upper Denton Chapel

Edenhall Church

EDENHALL   *St Cuthbert*   NY 569321

The nave has a blocked Norman north window. The imitation Norman chancel arch is of 1834. The chancel has a blocked Norman doorway and a 14th century east end. Of the 15th century are several windows and the low west tower with a window with shields and a projecting top with a small stone spire. The east window contains 14th century stained glass and there are further old fragments in the south windows. Some stalls have early 16th century linenfold panelling. The communion rail is 17th century. There are brasses to William Stapildon, d1458, and his wife, his figure being rather taller than hers. There are also several tablets to the Musgraves of Edenhall.

EGREMONT   *St Mary*   NY 011105

The present large church of 1880-1 designed by T.Lewis Banks incorporates fragments of the medieval church in the transept arches and the shafted lancets of the chancel. The west doorway has been re-erected in the churchyard and near it are sculptured fragments. Excavations in 1881 revealed footings of the Norman church and showed that the 13th century chancel had a contemporary north chapel.

Old print of windows at Egremont

ENNERDALE BRIDGE   *St Mary*

NY 068158

The neo-Norman church of 1856-8 and 1885 incorporates some genuine Norman parts in the south doorway and the chancel arch with one scalloped capital.

FARLAM   *St Thomas*   NY 568598

Until rebuilt by Salvin in 1859 the church had a nave and narrower chancel.

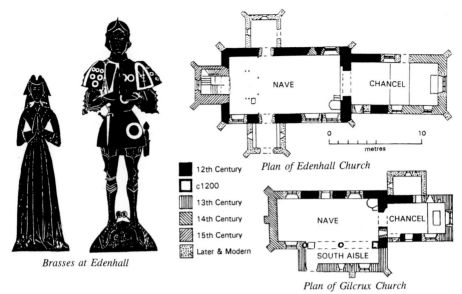

12th Century

c1200

13th Century

14th Century

15th Century

Later & Modern

Brasses at Edenhall

Plan of Edenhall Church

Plan of Gilcrux Church

GILCRUX   *St Mary*   NY 117383

The single stepped chancel arch on plain imposts and the blocked chancel doorway are Norman. The Late Norman south arcade has two arches with a slight chamfer on one order. The west respond is actually a full pier, evidence that the aisle was, or was intended to be, longer than it is now. The nave west end is 14th century. The windows are of various periods. There are two fragments of and Anglo-Danish cross.

GLASSONBY   *St Michael*   NY 577390

The medieval church was destroyed by the River Eden and a new church was built further east in the late 17th century. The nave south windows could be of that date, although their arches are later. The chancel windows look like reused medieval work. There is a hogback coffin lid in the porch and two pieces of a 9th century cross with interlace and vine scrolls. Fragments of a later cross lie outside nearby.

GOSFORTH   *St Mary*   NY 073037

The 14th century chancel arch stands on reset Norman columns with capitals carved on one side with a green man and on the other with three heads. Also Norman are the roll-moulded south doorway and the base of the nave walls. The church was remodelled in 1789 and a transept added in 1858, but the nave, chancel, north aisle and vestries are now mostly of Ferguson's rebuilding of 1896-7. Inside are two hogback tomb-stones, one with a battle scene, the other having a Crucifix on one side and a figure on the other. There are three Saxon cross-heads and fragments of shafts with interlace, a dragon, and two men in a boat with many fishes. There are several old coffin lids including one with a cross and leaf scrolls and tiny shears. Outside is the famous late 10th century cross 4.5m high. The shaft starts off round and then becomes a slender square. On the east face below Christ with outstretched arms are two men, one with a sword, the other with a lance. Above is plaiting with a beast's head and then a wheel-head. There are other scenes with fighting men on the other faces perhaps illustrating moments recalled in the Nordic sagas. See p48.

Interior of Grasmere Church

GRASMERE   *St Oswald*   NY 337074

As the walls are rendered outside and whitewashed inside and the windows are mostly Victorian this is not an easy building to date. The wide nave and the tower with a battered base are probably 14th century, and perhaps also the chancel. There is one original window with a trefoiled head west of the porch. The wide Langdale Aisle on the north side has an arcade of five unmoulded pointed arches on square piers probably of the 1560s. John Benson of Baisbrowne's will of 1562 leaves money "so that the Roofe be taken down and maide oop again". The roof spans both nave and aisle but is divided into two with kingposts on either side of an upper arcade of round arches set above the spandrels of the lower ones. This upper arcade supports the collar beam and is probably slightly later. One bench at the west end is dated 1635. The almsbox is dated 1648. The sanctuary chairs are inscribed T.L. 1677 and M.B. 1707. The many Fleming family monuments include a tablet to Daniel, d1701. There is also a tablet to the celebrated poet William Wordsworth, d1850, whose grave lies outside. The fragment of a slim shaft with foliage, a beast and a figure is probably 12th century. The font is said to be from Furness Abbey.

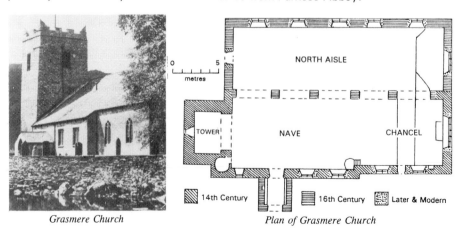

Grasmere Church   *Plan of Grasmere Church*

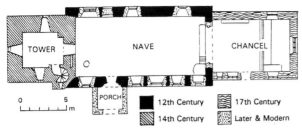

Plan of Great Salkeld Church

Doorway, Great Salkeld

GREAT SALKELD *St Cuthbert* NY 552368

The late 14th century tower is embattled with a higher stair turret. It has a tunnel vaulted lowest stage only entered through a doorway closed by a yett, and the level above that has a fireplace, so the tower could have formed a residence or a refuge against raids. The fine Norman south doorway has three orders of columns, capitals with beasts, human heads a trails running onto the abaci, and chevrons on the arches. The neo-Norman nave windows are of 1866 and the chancel windows are probably 17th century. There is an effigy of the priest Thomas de Caldebec, d1320.

Great Salkeld Church

GREYSTOKE   *St Andrew*   NY 444308

The chancel arch responds are 13th century, and probably also the six bay arcades. The piers may be 17th century replacements and were heightened c1818. The eastern bays originally opened into transepts but these were later absorbed into wide aisles, making this one of the largest medieval churches in Cumbria. In 1382 the church was very decayed and the inhabitants of Threlkeld and Wethermeloch were compelled to contribute to the rebuilding on pain of excommunication. A college for six chantry priests and eight secular canons was founded here the same year. The aisle windows, 16th or 17th century, have round-headed lights, doubled in number and half the size in the heads. On the south side is a two storey late medieval vestry. A squint from the north aisle to the chancel is now blocked. The diagonally buttressed west tower was entirely rebuilt in 1848. An inscription declares "This chancel was repaired 1645 by Thomas Howard of Greystoke Earl of Arundel and Surrey and William Morland Rector" but it looks Victorian.

A late medieval screen with dainty tracery closes off the chancel. Some of the choir stalls have miserichords carved with motifs such as St Michael and the Dragon, two youths and a donkey, and a man mounting a horse. In the east window is 15th century glass depicting the story of St Andrew. An alabaster effigy of a knight of c1360 has angels by his pillow and a canopy over his head. Another alabaster effigy is of John, Lord Greystoke, c1436. Part of the tomb chest also remains. There are small brasses depicting the priest John de Whelpdale (upper half only), d1526, Margaret Moresby, d1528, Winifred Newport, d1547, and Richard Newport, d1551.

GRINSDALE   *St Kentigern*   NY 373581

The church lies beyond the village by a bend of the River Eden. It is of 1740 and has a tiny west tower, a three bay nave and a two bay chancel with arched windows.

Greystoke Church

Effigies at Greystoke

HAILE   *Dedication Unknown*   NY 030088

The church has Georgian plain arched windows but the walls are medieval. The west porch was added by Ferguson in 1882. A SE quoin is part of a Saxon cross-shaft with scrolls. Outside the west wall is a monument to John Ponsonby, d1670.

HARRINGTON   *St Mary*   NX 995257

Brass at Greystoke

The west tower is of 1905-7 but has a 17th century doorway towards the nave with a basket-arch. The octagonal font with intersecting arches on colonettes is dated 1634 but may be older. In the porch is a Norman capital carved with small figures. There is also part of an Anglo-Danish cross-shaft. The wide nave is said to be of 1885 but may actually be of 1811, when a new church was erected here.

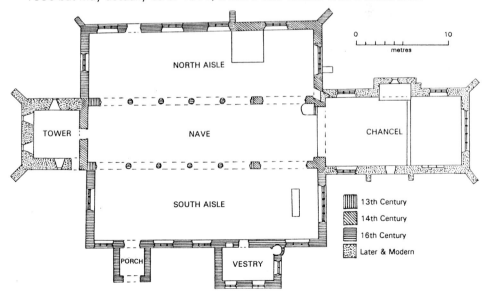

Plan of Greystoke Church

Interior of Hawkshead Church

HAWKSHEAD　*St Michael*　SD 352981

The church is a long, low rectangle lying on an eminence. It has aisles with rather shapeless piers and arches and a low west tower. The north aisle bears the date 1578, when work was done for Edwin Sandys, Archbishop of York. Much of the church could well be of that period, having rounded mouldings to the straight-headed windows, but the clerestory may be an addition, being dated 1633, whilst the south aisle has one 15th century window, and the north doorway jambs could be 13th century work reset. The internal walls are whitewashed with inscriptions of 1688 and 1711. The Sandys Chapel contains effigies of the Archbishop's parents, William Sandys and Mary Dixon, the tomb once being dated 1578. There is a monument by the tower arch to Daniel Rawlinson, founder of Hawkshead School Library in 1699.

HAYTON　*St Mary Magdalene*　NY 508577

The nave of five bays with arched, keyed-in windows and the thin west tower are of 1780. The Venetian window from the east wall was reset when a chancel was added in 1842. On the north side is an addition containing the raised family pew of the Grahams of Edmond Castle to whom there are many memorials.

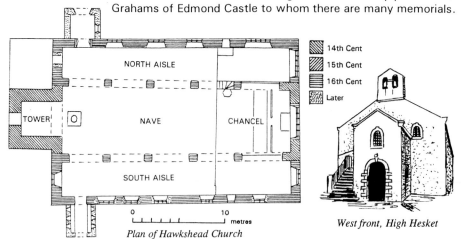

14th Cent
15th Cent
16th Cent
Later

NORTH AISLE

TOWER　　NAVE　　CHANCEL

SOUTH AISLE

0　　　　10　metres

Plan of Hawkshead Church

West front, High Hesket

HELSINGTON   *St John*   SD 488889

The single chamber may have walling of 1726 hidden under the roughcasted exterior but the features are all of 1898 and 1910. The site is quite isolated.

HEVERSHAM   *St Peter*   SD 496834

The north arcade is Victorian but the south arcade retains late 12th century piers (one with a waterleaf capital) and an east respond with crockets. The north chapel with a two bay arcade is early 16th century but contains a reset window of c1300 with cusped intersected tracery and has a screen of 1605. The aisles have 15th century windows, partly restored. The west tower is of 1869-70 by Paley & Austin and the clerestory lancets are also Victorian. The south door has 13th century ironwork. There is a fragment of a late 9th century cross-shaft with scrolls, grapes, and pairs of birds and beasts, and also an urn in a recess to Anna Preston, d1767.

Heversham Church

HIGHHEAD   *Dedication Unknown*   NY 406436

This chapel in a field near Highhead Castle is dated 1682 and is now a private residence. It has one mullioned window and others with pointed arches.

HIGH HESKET   *St Mary*   NY 476444

The chancel arch is 13th or 14th century. The double bellcote is probably 17th century and there is an 18th century west porch. The keyed-in arched windows of the nave are of 1720 and the east window and north aisle are Victorian. Inside is a monument to Bernard Kirkbride, d1677. The Parker mausoleum lies in the churchyard.

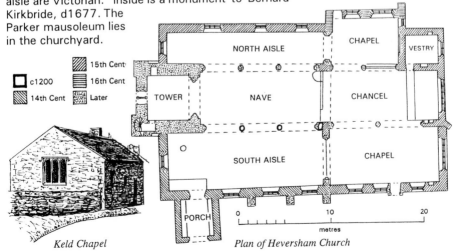

Keld Chapel   *Plan of Heversham Church*

HOLME ST CUTHBERT   *St Cuthbert*   NY 104471

The church is of 1845 by William Armstrong and has a west tower with a stair turret of 1924 but it contains two defaced pieces of an effigy of a 14th century knight. The sea NW of here is said to have washed away two former churches.

HUTTON-IN-THE-FOREST   *St James*   NY 459365

The church was built in 1714 but has been remodelled or rebuilt, It contains a 17th century communion rail and a fragment of a cross-shaft with interlace.

HUTTON ROOF   *St John*   SD 569788

The present church with a north aisle and a porch tower on the south side was built in 1881-2 to a design by Austin & Paley. All that remains of a church built here in 1757 is the bellcote re-erected in the vicarage garden.

INGS   *St Anne*   SD 445986

This church erected in 1743 at the expense of rich Leghorn merchant Robert Bateman, who was born here, comprises a west tower and a main body with a Venetian east window with the top reaching into a broken pediment. The arched side windows have keystones. The coved ceiling is probably of 1878-9 when a north transept was added. The font has four large cherubs' heads.

IREBY   *Dedication Unknown*   NY 224394

Two octagonal piers are the only remains of a nave with a three bay north aisle and a south porch demolished in 1848. The Norman chancel is cared for by the Churches Conservation Trust. It has three original east windows and traces of two more on the south. The north window and blocked north doorway look 13th century and the roof is 18th century. The new church of St James built in 1847 in the village 1.5km to the east contains a Norman font, a slab to John de Ireby and some carved stones.

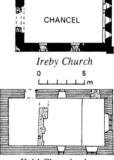

Ireby Church

0   5
└─┴─┴─┴─┴─┘ m

Keld Chapel: plan

Ings Church

Ireby Church

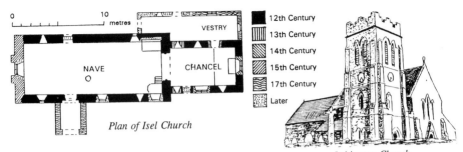

Plan of Isel Church

Irthington Church

IRTHINGTON   *St Kentigern*   NY 499617

The arcades of round arches with one step and one slight chamfer set on round piers with leaf capital and square abaci are of the 1170s. The 13th century chancel arch has two orders of columns with spurs and crocket capitals. The chancel masonry is also probably 13th century but the rest of the exterior is of 1849-53 by Bloxham with a NW tower beyond the north aisle added in 1897.

IRTON   *St Paul*   NY 092005

The church is of 1856-7 by Miles Thompson, but the chancel was enlarged in 1873. In the churchyard is a 9th century cross-shaft still 3m high including the head. There are vine-scrolls on the edges, interlace, frets and rosettes.

ISEL   *St Michael*   NY 164334

The nave and chancel each have Norman windows on both sides and original doorways, that on the south side of the nave having one order of columns with scalloped capitals and chevrons in the arch. The chancel arch has a roll moulding with quarter-hollows. One south window has been altered in the 18th century. A fragment of an Anglo-Danish cross-shaft is adorned with a rounded swastika and other motifs.

KELD   *No Dedication Known*   NY 554145

This is a small 16th century chapel-of-ease with a three light east window, A two-light window and a single light window in each side wall, and a door on the north now opening into a west end which has been divided off later by a wall.

Isel Church

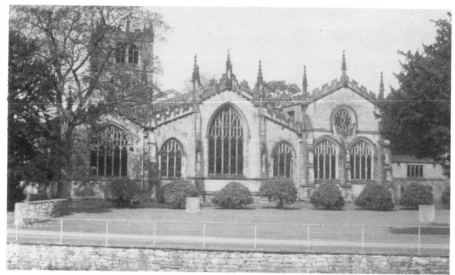

East front of Kendal Church

KENDAL   *Holy Trinity*   SD 516922

The church forms a large rectanguler of unusual width. It has an undivided nave and chancel which are fully aisled with arcades of eight bays, plus an extra ninth bay where the aisles flank the tower. The three eastern arches of the nave arcades are 13th century and the chancel arcades are Victorian, the easternmost bays of the aisles here being screened off as chapels. The 15th century piers at the west end have no capitals. This then was the shape and size of the church at the end of the 15th century. In the 16th century wide outer aisles and chapels were added to both sides, the Bellingham aisle on the north being spacious enough to be a substantial church in its own right. It has some original bosses remaining in the ribbed ceiling. Externally some original details remain on the west and north sides of the church, but on the east and south sides all the buttresses and windows were renewed in the 1850s, and a porch was added west of the outer south aisle.

The oldest feature inside is a fragment of a 9th century cross-shaft with grapes and leaves. The octagonal black marble font with concave sides and shields is late 15th century. The inner south chapel has an early 16th century screen and a fragment of 15th century glass. There are stalls with carved arms and benches and stalls with 16th century poppy-heads. There are many tablets in the nave and aisles. In the Bellingham Chapel is a late 13th century coffin lid with a foliated cross and a sword and shield. On a tomb chest are Victorian brasses of Sir Roger Bellingham, d1533 and his wife. A brass of Alan Bellingham, d1577, is fixed to a wall. In the south chapel is a 16th century tomb chest with a few shields and there is a similar one in the outer south chapel. There is also a tomb with Tuscan supports and a damaged effigy of Walter Strickland, d1656. See page 63.

KENTMERE   *St Cuthbert*   NY 456041

The roof beams are 16th century but the walls were rebuilt in 1866 and there was a remodelling in the 1950s. The church has a single chamber with a west tower.

Interior of Kendal Church

CHAPEL

NORTH AISLE

CHAPEL

TOWER

NAVE

SOUTH AISLE

CHAPEL

PORCH

CHAPEL

Plan of Kendal Church

KILLINGTON   *All Saints*   SD 614890

The single chamber has 14th or 15th century windows on the north side and 17th century windows on the south side. There is a late 18th century marble tablet.

KIRKANDREWS   *St Andrews*   NY 391720

This is a proud ashlar-faced building of 1776 with a west tower crowned by an open rotunda of columns at the bell-stage and a stone cap. There is a Tuscan west doorway with a pediment and there is another pediment above. The east wall has a large window flanked by niches.

KIRKBAMPTON   *St Peter*   NY 305565

This is a Norman church with a north doorway with one order of columns, a tympanum with a small figure of an ecclesiastic in one corner, and an arch with chevrons with a hood-mould with huge billets. The south doorway is also original but very decayed, but the priest's doorway in the chancel has a tympanum with bands of lozenges using different coloured stones. The chancel arch has a roll and one step and lies on responds with scallop capitals with fish-scale patterns on the abaci. Two small original round-headed windows remain, one now reset in the organ chamber.

KIRKBRIDE   *St Bride*   NY 230574

The church is Norman and has plain north and south doorways, plus a chamfered priest's doorway now leading into a Victorian vestry. There are recesses on either side of the plain unmoulded chancel arch. Two north windows are original, several others being Victorian. There is a square 13th century font with dog-tooth and fleurons and also a larger later medieval font with nobbly leaves and circles with trefoils and quatrefoils. See page 5.

Norman chancel arch at Kirkbampton

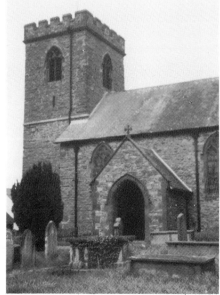

Kirkby Ireleth Church

Kirkbride Church

KIRKBY IRELETH   *St Cuthbert*   SD 234822

The chancel has two Norman windows, that on the south side now blocked, and the spacious nave has a fine Norman south doorway with two orders of columns with decorated scallops and waterleaves on the capitals, and beak-heads on one of the arches. The west tower was rebuilt in 1829 and the windows are all renewed. The north aisle and arcade have also been mostly rebuilt but a squint survives. The chancel windows have fragments of medieval glass including a 14th century seated Christ. The octagonal goblet-shaped font with one shield on the stem is late medieval. There is a 13th century cross-slab to Alexander de Kirkby by the nave SE window.

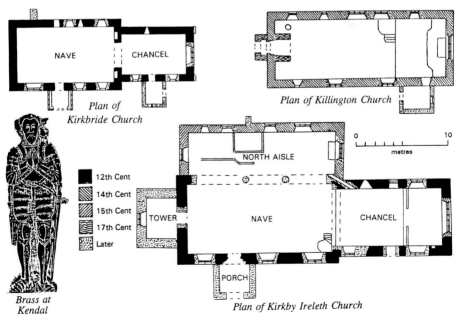

Plan of Kirkbride Church

Plan of Killington Church

NAVE

CHANCEL

NORTH AISLE

TOWER   NAVE   CHANCEL

PORCH

0   10
metres

■ 12th Cent
▨ 14th Cent
▧ 15th Cent
▨ 17th Cent
▨ Later

Brass at Kendal

Plan of Kirkby Ireleth Church

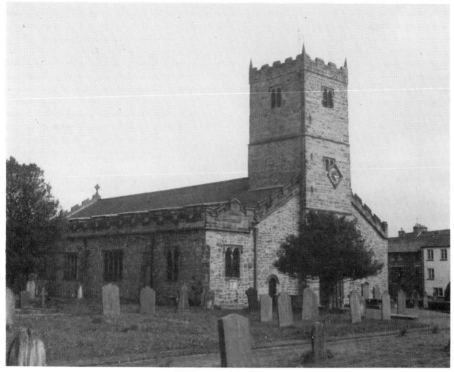

Kirkby Lonsdale Church

KIRKBY LONSDALE   *St Mary*   NY 611788

The nave is only 4m wide and has on the north side a massive arcade of roll-moulded arches of c1110-5 with round piers with incised trellis patterns like those of Durham Cathedral set either side of a compound pier. The ambitious intended scheme seems to have been abandoned and work only resumed in the late 12th century with the erection of the south arcade of chamfered round arches on round and octagonal piers and the west tower with a fine west doorway. This has two orders of shafts with reeded capitals and arches carved with saltire crosses with motifs inside including an archer and a dragon. In c1200 the arcades were continued eastwards making a total of seven bays and an east wall built with slightly stepped triple lancets. Possibly this part replaced a church existing before c1110 which had remained in use whilst the new works remained incomplete. The position of the west lancets shows that the original aisles were narrow. They were widened in the 14th century and given windows with reticulated tracery at the east end. The priest's doorway is work of c1200 reset and there is reset Norman work with chevrons and a roll rood-mould over the main south dorway, now covered by a porch of 1866. Several south windows are of c1400. In the 16th century an outer north aisle was added with windows of four round-headed lights under square heads with hood-moulds. Older windows were reused in the aisle west end, and the east end is 18th century work incorporating a doorway and two windows of the 16th century. The tower top is dated 1705 and has pairs of round arched lights.

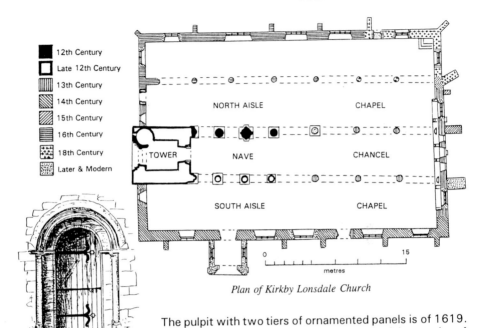

Legend:
- ■ 12th Century
- □ Late 12th Century
- ▦ 13th Century
- ▨ 14th Century
- ▧ 15th Century
- ▤ 16th Century
- ▨ 18th Century
- ▒ Later & Modern

TOWER NORTH AISLE CHAPEL NAVE CHANCEL SOUTH AISLE CHAPEL

0 15

metres

Plan of Kirkby Lonsdale Church

*Priest's Doorway,
Kirkby Lonsdale*

The pulpit with two tiers of ornamented panels is of 1619. The cupboard in the west end of the north aisle may be of the same period, perhaps with older panels. There are many tablets plus a bigger monument to Hugh Ashton, d1749.

Interior of Kirkby Lonsdale Church

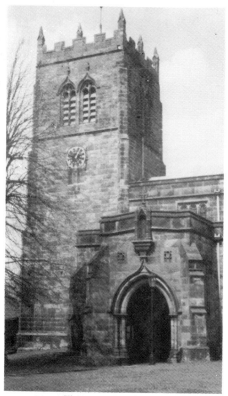

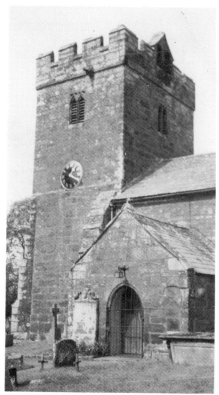

Kirkby Stephen Church

Kirkby Thore Church

KIRKBY STEPHEN   *St Stephen*   NY 775088

In 1847 Robert Carpenter rebuilt the chancel and its north and south chapels, the south transept except for a 14th century doorway, the clerestory and the outer wall of the narrow north aisle. At the west end of this aisle is a short length of thick Norman walling with a 14th century window pierced through it. There is also a fine Norman capital of c1175 carved with leaves lying loose in the church. Of the 13th century are the north transept with clasping buttresses and two west lancets, the arch from the crossing to the south transept, a corbel in the south chapel with a chevron pattern, and the arcades of seven bays with double chamfered arches on circular piers with waterholding bases and octagonal abaci. For some reason the easternmost bay is only half as wide as the others. The wide south aisle with several three-light windows is 15th century. The south porch is Victorian. The diagonally buttressed west tower with a very high arch towards the nave is 16th century.

The north transept has a screen made up of old parts including 17th century balusters and 16th century Flamboyant tracery. There are several fragments of cross-slabs, one having interlace and a bearded, bound figure, and there is a hogback grave-stone with a tiled roof pattern. In the south chapel is a 15th century tomb chest with an effigy of one of the Musgraves. The tomb chest in a coarsely foliated gable in the chapel south wall is of Richard Musgrave, d1674. In the north chapel is a tomb chest with effigies of Thomas, 1st Lord Wharton, d1568, and his two wives.

KIRKBY THORE

St Michael NY 638260

The nave, the chancel with one altered original window, and the rectangular west tower are all Norman. All these parts have 14th century windows. The porch and the north aisle are also 14th century although the two bay arcade with a quatrefoil shaped pier may be late 13th century. The chancel was lengthened in the 13th century and two of the south windows were blocked up in the 17th century. The chancel arch has original Norman imposts, reset since the arch has been widened. Of 1688 is the octagonal font with a coat of arms. The pulpit with caryatids at the corners and arched panels is dated 1631. The communion rail is inscribed A.R.Caroli II 35, meaning the 35th year of Charles II's reign taken as beginning in 1649.

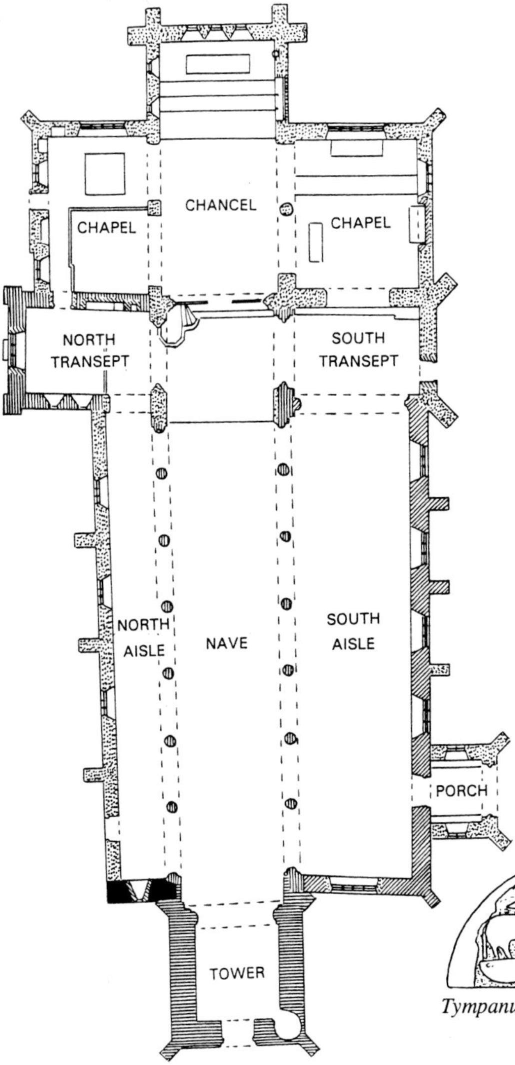

Plan of Kirkby Stephen Church

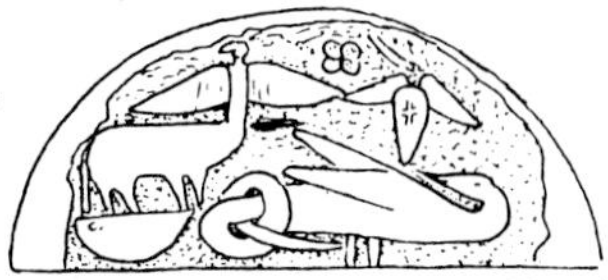

Tympanum at Kirkby Thore Church

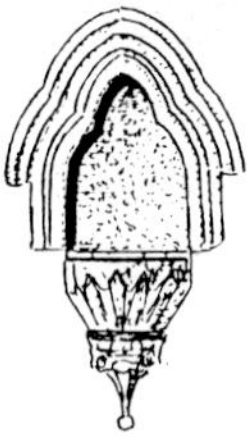

Piscina at Kirkby Stephen

Stone at Kirkby Stephen

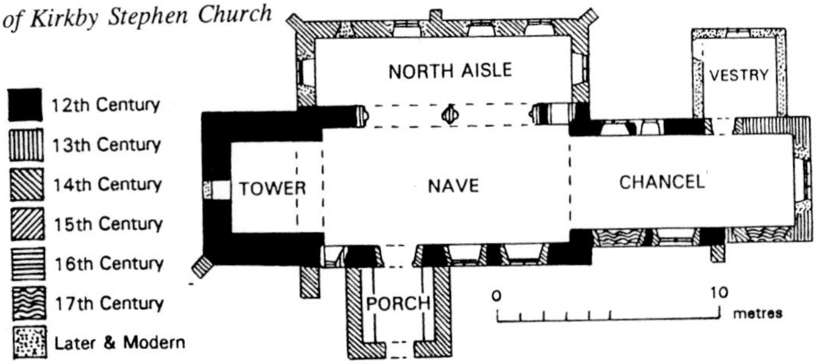

■	12th Century
▦	13th Century
▨	14th Century
▧	15th Century
▤	16th Century
▥	17th Century
▦	Later & Modern

Plan of Kirkby Thore Church

KIRKCAMBECK   *St Kentigern*   NY 534689

East of the church of 1885 is an arch built of stones from the old church on this site.

KIRKLAND   *St Lawrence*   NY 072180

The features are mostly of the rebuilding of 1880 but the pointed-trefoiled piscina and the triple-chamfered chancel arch suggest a date for the walls of c1280-1300. There is also an effigy of a knight of about that period or slightly earlier. In the churchyard is a Saxon cross still complete with the free-armed head with holes between arms.

KIRKLINTON   *St Cuthbert*   NY 433671

The church is entirely of 1845 except for some reused Norman parts in the tower arch. Other old parts lie outside and there are two piers and capitals in the rectory garden. There are monuments to Edward & Dorothy Appleby, both d1698, Joseph Dacre Appleby, d1729, and Joseph Dacre Appleby, d1738.

KIRKOSWALD   *St Oswald*   NY 555408

The chancel arch stands on Norman bases, and there is a Norman two bay south arcade of round arches. The north arcade is perhaps of c1200, the arches still being round but with chamfers. A 13th century doorway was reset on the south side in the 14th century when the aisles were widened, lengthened westwards along with an extra bay added to the nave, and chapels were added either side of the chancel. The arches to the chapels from the aisles now open into shallow Victorian bays since the chapels were dismantled when a wide new chancel was erected to serve a college of six priests founded by Thomas, Lord Dacre c1523. The chancel has a five light east window and pairs of tall straight-headed three-light side windows with round-arched lights. The north aisle has one late 15th century window but is otherwise mostly rebuilt. The church has no bellcote or tower and the bells lie instead in a tower of 1897 on top of the adjacent hill. This replaces a wooden campanile of 1747. There are several coffin lids with foliated crosses outside the church. Inside are many tablets to the Fetherstonhaughs of The College and a monument of 1609 to members of the Brougham and Bertram families, with kneeling figures.

Kirkoswald Church

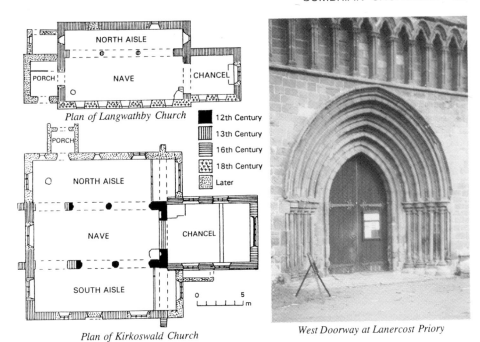

Plan of Langwathby Church

■	12th Century
▤	13th Century
▦	16th Century
▨	18th Century
▧	Later

Plan of Kirkoswald Church

West Doorway at Lanercost Priory

LAMPLUGH   *St Michael*   NY 089208

The church is of 1870 by Butterfield but incorporates old doorways in the chancel and vestry and one 15th century window.

Langwathby Church

Lanercost Priory Church

LANERCOST   *St Mary Magdalene*   NY 556637

Robert de Vaux founded a priory of Augustinian canons here beside the River Ithing in 1160. By 1169 it was possible to consecrate part of the church, although the earliest surviving feature is the west doorway of the south transept of the 1180s or 90s. The present east end, now ruined but standing to full height, is of the 1220s. It comprises a chancel four bays long with three east lancets of even height with three stepped ones above. Chapels flank the western two bays, and there are outer chapels forming east aisles to the transepts. There is a clerestory with hood-moulded lancets. Over the crossing is a plain tower. These parts and what remains of the buildings around the cloister are in the care of English Heritage. Only the nave remains in use as a parish church. It has an aisle on the north side only. The arcade consists of three bays of triple chamfered 13th century arches on octagonal piers, then a short piece of wall against which was set the pulpitum, and then one further east arch. The cloister abutted the south side so there are no windows there below the level of the clerestory. Despite an unevenness of the buttresses, the west front is a fine composition with a frieze of pointed-trefoil headed arcading over a big portal with four orders of columns with nailhead on the moulded capitals, fillets on the arch rolls and dog-tooth on the hood-mould. Above is a tall group of three stepped lancets connected by a shafted arcade with shaft-rings. The statue of St Mary Magdalene in the gable is of the 1260s, dating the completion of work gradually progressing from the east end to the west. Slight differences in the nave clerestory gallery indicate pauses in construction, dogtooth and nailhead appearing towards the west.

Part of a cross which stood north of the nave lies in the aisle. It has dog-tooth and Roman lettering. In the eastern parts lie three tomb chests, one with an inscription referring to Thomas, Lord Dacre, who took over the priory when it was dissolved in 1536. Another is 15th century but lies under an earlier segmental canopy with dog-ooth. Several 19th century monuments lie in the north transept.

LANGWATHBY *St Peter* NY 569338

Externally this is a church of 1718 with a five bay nave and a two bay chancel with long round-arched windows and quoins. The porch is of 1836 and the east window may be still later. Inside is a rather restored 13th century north arcade of three bays.

LAZONBY *St Nicholas* NY 569399

The church is of 1863 by Anthony Salvin. There is a plain shaft of a medieval churchyard cross standing 2m high.

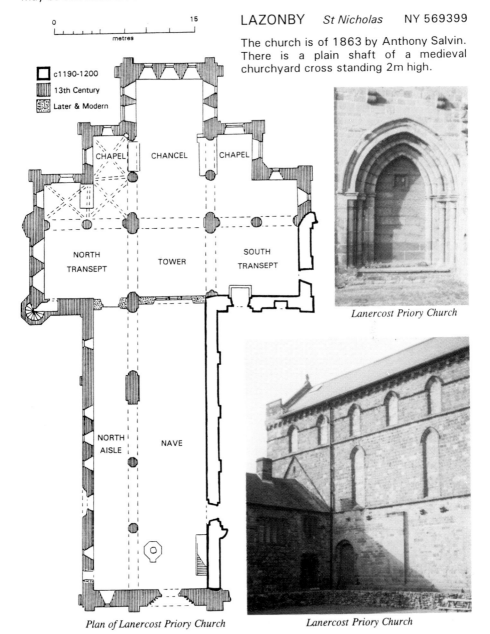

0   15
metres

☐ c1190-1200
▥ 13th Century
▨ Later & Modern

CHAPEL   CHANCEL   CHAPEL

NORTH TRANSEPT   TOWER   SOUTH TRANSEPT

NORTH AISLE   NAVE

Plan of Lanercost Priory Church

Lanercost Priory Church

Lanercost Priory Church

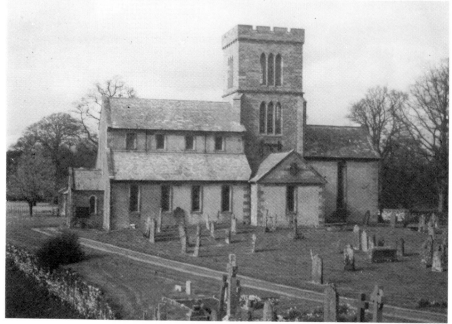

Lowther Church

LONG MARTON   *St Margaret & St James*   NY 666240

The large quoins of the nave and the south doorway with a tympanum carved with
a dragon, a winged beast, and a shield and sword suggest a late 11th century date.
The small north window may also be of that date. The north doorway, the west
tower and the chancel are from later in the Norman period. The piscina, sedilia, east
and south windows, the priest's doorway are of the 14th century, when the south
transept and vestry were also added.

LOWTHER   *St Michael*   NY 519244

The four bay north arcade of c1165-75 has single stepped arches on circular piers
with square abaci and capitals with either foliage or many scallops. The south arcade
of c1200 still has round arches, but with chamfers and smaller octagonal piers. East
of these is a crossing of c1210-30 with triple shafts, the middle ones keeled, and the
arches from the aisles into the transepts are of the same period. These internal details
come as rather a surprise for the outer walls of the nave, aisles, transepts and
chancel were rebuilt in 1686 by Sir John Lowther. The high central tower is partly
his work also, but the dome and lantern he provided were removed in 1856. The
west porch and the NE vestry are Victorian. See pages 4 & 12.

   The communion rail with twisted balusters is of c1690, as is probably also the
baluster font. The pulpit is 18th century. In the porch are some hogback coffins. In
the south transept is an effigy of Sir Richard Lowther, d1608, and a semi-reclining
figure of John, Viscount Lonsdale, d1700. There are also busts of Sir John Lowther,
d1637 and Sir John Lowther, d1675, both of the latter date. In the north transept are
several later monuments and outside is the Lowther Mausoleum of 1857.

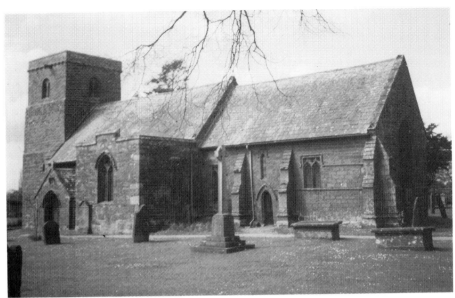

Long Marton Church

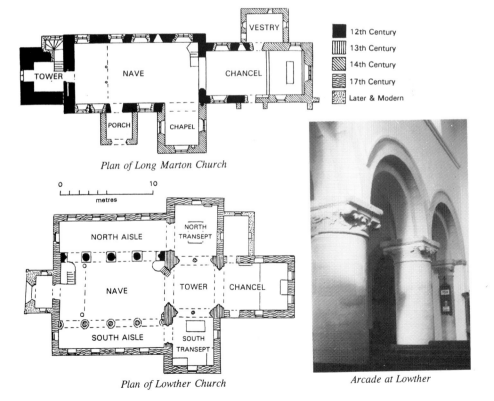

■	12th Century
▥	13th Century
▨	14th Century
▦	17th Century
▦	Later & Modern

Plan of Long Marton Church

Plan of Lowther Church

Arcade at Lowther

LUPTON   *All Saints*   NY 567809

The small neo-Norman church of 1867 contains a font from Kirkby Lonsdale supposedly of 1686 but not looking like a work of that period.

MARYPORT   *St Mary*   NY 037366

Only the baluster font remains from a chapel-of-ease built here in 1760. The church was rebuilt in 1847 but only the tower is of that period as there was another rebuilding in 1890-2 to a design by J.H.Martindale.

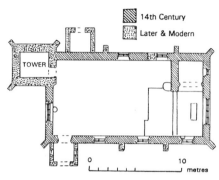

Plan of Melmerby Church

MARTINDALE   *St Martin*   NY 435184

This remotely sited single chamber amongst the mountains was built in 1634. It has plain oblong windows. The pulpit with initials of John Dawes, the benches and some panelling are of the same date. The floor may have been of earth until the present flagstones were laid in 1724. The present roof is modern, the original having collapsed on the same day in 1882 that the new church to the NE was consecrated. This new church lies in a more central location for the parish and was designed in a simple lancet style by J.A.Cory.

Melmerby Church

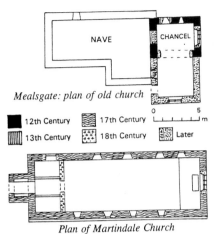

Mealsgate: plan of old church

■ 12th Century   17th Century

▓ 13th Century   18th Century   Later

0   5
m

Mealsgate Old Church

Plan of Martindale Church

MATTERDALE   *Dedication Unknown*   NY 396225

The single chamber with plain mullioned windows and a king-post roof could be of 1573 when the church was licensed, but there is a datestone of 1686 with the initials G.S. The tiny west tower was added in 1848. Probably of the 1680s are the plain benches and the communion rail, whilst the pulpit and tester are 18th century. There is a studded door and a baluster font. A late medieval font lies nearby.

MEALSGATE   *All Hallows*   NY 204419

The church of 1896-9 designed by Ferguson at Leesrigg contains two old grave slabs. Of the old church near Whitehall the only roofed parts are the tiny Norman chancel and a south chapel added by Launcelot Salkeld in the 1580s but rebuilt in the 1860s. A monument lies against the blocked chancel arch. The nave walls are much ruined and reduced and the space within them filled with earth and rubbish.

MELMERBY   *St John Baptist*   NY 611375

The NW tower is of 1848 and so is much of the rest, but the walling is mostly 14th century and two late medieval north windows were reopened in 1928 when a gallery was removed. An arcade has been taken out, throwing the nave and aisle into one, but the NE corner is still divided off as a vestry. There are several old grave slabs.

Martindale Old Church

Milburn Church

Milburn Church

MILBURN   *St Cuthbert*   NY 652291

The nave and chancel both appear to be Norman and in the west wall is a reset stone with saltire crosses. The original south doorway with one order of columns is reset in a 14th century south aisle with an arcade of two bays with a quarefoil-shaped pier. Behind the altar is some 17th century panelling.

MILLOM   *Holy Trinity*   SD 162814

The old church lies beside the castle and there is a new church of Holy Trinity built in 1874 by Paley & Austin in the town. The old church has Norman north and south doorways and a window of that period in the chancel. In the 13th century a south aisle was added with three bays of arches on circular piers with octagonal abaci. The aisle was widened in the 14th century, one south window having flowing tracery and the west window being almond-shaped. The arcade west repond is also of that period. The low blocked arch in the nave west wall suggests that there was once a tower. Much of the exterior was restored in the 19th century. The communion rail contains work of c1630 and there are box pews. On a tomb chest are alabaster effigies of Sir John Hudleston, d1494, and his wife. There is a second somewhat later tomb chest with coarse shields and also a standing monument with pilasters and a pediment to Sir Joseph Huddlestone, d1700, and his wife Bridget, d1714.

Millom Church

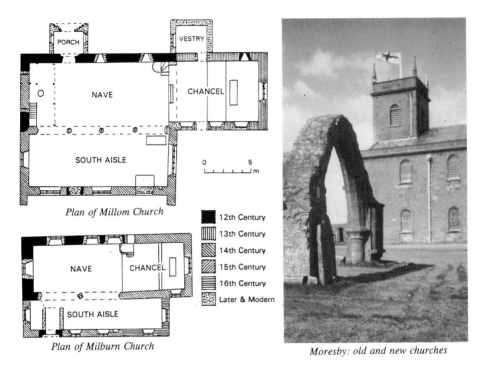

Plan of Millom Church

12th Century
13th Century
14th Century
15th Century
16th Century
Later & Modern

Plan of Milburn Church

Moresby: old and new churches

MORESBY   *St Bridget*   NX 983210

In the churchyard lies the chancel arch of the old church with semi-circular responds. The new church has a west tower and nave of 1822-3 with two tiers of arched windows. The chancel with a Venetian window and the internal details are of 1885.

Morland Church

MORLAND   *St Lawrence*   NY 598226

The west tower is Saxon work of the 11th century with a tall narrow doorway to the nave and bell-openings with a mid-wall shaft. The top stage is 17th century and the lead spire still later. At the end of the 12th century were built arcades of four bays of pointed arches with circular and octagonal piers. The east responds go with the transepts of the 1220s with double chamfered lancets and stop-chamfered buttresses. There is dog-tooth ornamentation on the south transept windows. Of the same period is the outer wall of the south aisle (which varies in width) with the south doorway adorned with shafts and rolls. The chancel may have some walling of c1300 but is essentially early 16th century with four-light windows to the east and south. Until then there was also a south chapel. The blocked arch of c1300 to it remains in the south transept. A similar chapel on the north side was rebuilt when the vestry was added by the Victorians. The south porch is 17th century but the outer arch is older, and the north aisle with typical Georgian arched windows with keystones is of 1758. The west walls of both aisles are 19th century. See page 77.

The small font with a contemporary cover with inscriptions is of 1662. The pulpit is 18th century. The top rail survives of a 14th or 15th century screen with nine male heads and a bust of an angel. The communion rail is mid 17th century. Also old are the benches with knobs and panelling against the west wall. In the south transept is a 13th century coffin lid with a foliated cross. A brass inscription to John Blythe, d1562, shows a knight of c1520 on the reverse side.

Musgrave: brass

IIII Saxon

||||| 13th Century

14th Century

16th Century

17th Century

18th Century

Later & Modern

0   10
metres

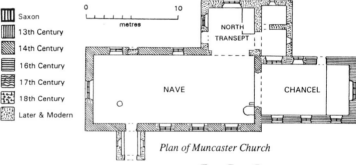

NORTH
TRANSEPT

NAVE

CHANCEL

Plan of Muncaster Church

*Morland: Reverse
of Blythe Brass*

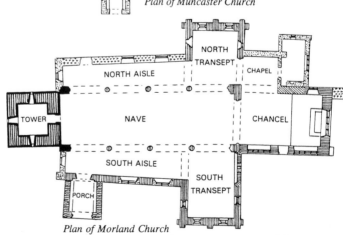

NORTH
TRANSEPT

NORTH AISLE

CHAPEL

TOWER

NAVE

CHANCEL

SOUTH AISLE

SOUTH
TRANSEPT

PORCH

Plan of Morland Church

Muncaster Church

MOSSER   *St Michael*   NY 114248

The doorway and windows of the small nave and chancel of 1773 are plain oblongs.

MUNCASTER   *St Michael*   SD 104966

The chancel has early 16th century windows. The nave windows are probably later 16th century but the masonry could be much older. The south porch, the north transept and the vestry are Victorian. In the churchyard is a cross-shaft with plainting. A wheel-head lies next to it. The first Lord Muncaster in the late 18th century put up plates to his ancestors in a fake ancient script.

MUNGRISDALE   *St Kentigern*   NY 364305

The single chamber of 1756 has arched windows with keystones. The pulpit of the same period contains older parts, one panel being dated 1679. Some of the box pews also look late 17th century.

MUSGRAVE   *St Theobald*   NY 767133

The church lies by the Eden below Great Musgrave and is of 1845 by G.R. Appleby. It contains a late 13th century coffin lid with a foliated cross and sword, and also a small brass depicting a priest of c1500 with an inscription across his chest.

Mungrisdale Church

Newton Reigny Church

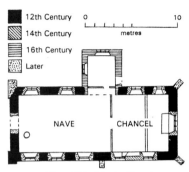

Plan of Newbiggin Church

NEWBIGGIN   *St Edmund*   NY 628287

The nave and chancel have 14th century windows but the walling is Norman, with a flat buttress at the west end and a pillar piscina. The east window contains fragments of 14th and 15th century stained glass. The north chapel is 16th century.

NEWTON ARLOSH   *St John Baptist*   NY 198553

This church was built under the terms of a licence of 1304. It was intended to be defensible, having a vaulted tower with a turret on corbels at the top, and originally only entered through a narrow doorway with a drawbar slot. The modest single chamber has small windows in the east and south walls. The octagonal font is probably original. By 1844 the church too small for the congregation and a big new chamber twice the size of the original was added on the north side. It has lancet windows. An apse was added on the east side of this extension in 1894.

NEWTON REIGNY   *St John*   NY 480315

The three bay south arcade with round piers, round abaci and pointed arches with slight chamfers and the chancel arch are of c1200. The north arcade with octagonal piers and full chamfers is early 13th century. The short chancel of 1876 by Ewan Christian is higher than the nave. There is a bellcote on the nave.

Newton Arlosh Church

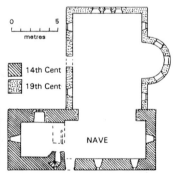

Plan of Newton Arlosh Church

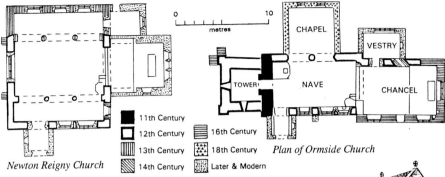

■ 11th Century	
▢ 12th Century	▦ 16th Century
▥ 13th Century	▦ 18th Century
▨ 14th Century	▩ Later & Modern

Newton Reigny Church

Plan of Ormside Church

OLD HUTTON   *St John Baptist*   SD 560887

The small nave and apse are of 1873 by Brade & Smailes. Inside is a late 17th century almsbox formed from a baluster with a bowl and lid on top.

Orton Church

ORMSIDE   *St James*   NY 701177

In the 11th century the church consisted of a small nave with a tall doorway on the south and a square chancel. In the mid 12th century a short aisle was added on the north with a two bay arcade with stepped arches and a circular pier with a square abacus. About the same time a new west wall was built with a doorway in a thickening intended to carry a bellcote. The doorway now opens into a tower probably built in the 1190s with small windows and clasping buttresses. The chancel seems to have been lengthened at the same time but it was mostly rebuilt and enlarged to the south in the 16th century, the two light south windows either side of a priest's doorway being of that period. In the 18th century the aisle was replaced by the Helton Chapel. The porch, chancel arch, and vestry are Victorian, but there must have been a medieval vestry since a squint is provided from the present one. The 9th century Ormside Bowl, a fine piece of Saxon metalwork found in the churchyard in the early 19th century, is now in the York Museum.

Ormside Church

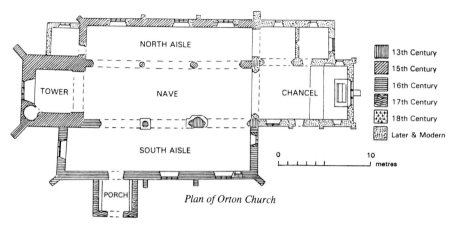

Plan of Orton Church

ORTON   *All Saints*   NY 623084

The diagonally buttressed west tower and the north aisle with a three bay arcade are late 15th century but the aisle windows are later. The early 16th century south aisle partly overlaps the tower south side. A 17th century porch now protects its doorway and there are original three-light windows. The arcade on this side has two 16th century bays and then a wider earlier bay, all that remains of a cruciform 13th century church apart from a trefoiled piscina in the eastern part of the aisle corresponding to the former south transept and the south respond of the former western arch of the crossing. The font is dated 1662 with initials, flowers, flowers and the head of Gothic window. Parts remain of a former Jacobean communion rail.

ORTON   *St Giles*   NY 329543

The chancel has two Norman windows and on the north side is a length of nailhead ornamentation. The nave was lengthened in the 18th century.

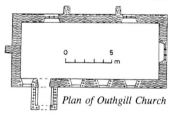

Plan of Outhgill Church

OUSBY   *St Luke*   NY 626346

The church lies some way east of the village. Its features are mostly of 1858 but the walling suggests a 12th century nave and chancel were each lengthened in the 14th century. Of that period are the sedilia and piscina and the fine wooden effigy of a cross-legged knight. The middle part of the nave north wall is perhaps 13th century.

OUTHGILL   *St Mary*   NY 786015

The north windows and the south doorway date from the time of work executed for the Lady Anne Clifford c1660 as recorded in an inscription over the porch. The south windows are of 1768 and the east window is 20th century. See page 11.

PENNINGTON   *St Michael*   SD 264774

The existing church was built in 1826 and was remodelled and extended in 1926. Reset in the south aisle is a Norman tympanum with a demi-figure of Christ with raised hands and a runic inscription referring to Gamel, founder of the church, and the mason Hubert who worked on it. There is also a Norman scallop capital in the porch.

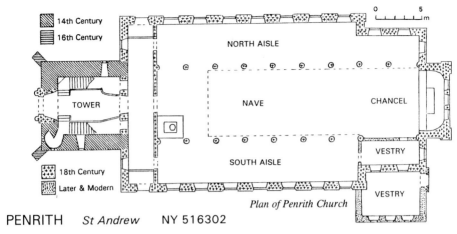

14th Century

16th Century

NORTH AISLE

0   5
m

TOWER

NAVE

CHANCEL

VESTRY

18th Century

Later & Modern

SOUTH AISLE

VESTRY

Plan of Penrith Church

PENRITH   *St Andrew*   NY 516302

This fine church of 1720-2 has eight bays with two tiers of round-arched windows separated by broad pilasters. Other pilasters at the corners are rusticated. The tower doorway with Tuscan columns, a triglyph frieze and pediment is an insertion, for the tower is medieval. It contains a staircase up to the galleries which are supported on Tuscan columns with other thin columns above. The chancel has two bays and ends in a Venetian window. The pulpit goes with the church, the chandelier was given in 1745, whilst the font is older, being dated 1661. One window on the north side has fragments of 15th century stained glass. In the tower are defaced effigies of Anthony Hutton and his wife, d1637, and a fine 13th century coffin lid with a foliated cross. See also page 84.

Penrith Church

Orton Church

Ousby Church

Outside to the north of Penrith church are four hogback coffins. Grouped with them are two crosses known at the Giant's Grave, and another called the Giant's Thumb, all three probably of c1000. They have square shafts which start off round. The west cross of the Giant's Grave has a small head and much interlace. The east cross has interlace and scenes of the Agnus Dei and a bound figure next to a woman with a serpent above. The other cross is shorter and again has interlace.

PLUMBLAND   *St Cuthbert*   NY 141392

The church is mostly of 1870-1 by Cory & Ferguson but retains from the 12th century a plain doorway reset in the porch and a fine chancel arch with tripartite responds, plus from the 13th century a pointed trefoil-headed piscina, a doorway into the vestry, and a lancet reset in the vestry. There are three fragments of a hogback tomb-stone with Anglo-Danish style dragons.

PONSONBY   *Dedication Unknown*   NY 043056

The church is of 1840 and 1874 but contains two coffin lids with crosses and a sword and shears plus a tablet to Thomas Curwen, d1653, with figures in relief.

Ravenstonedale Church

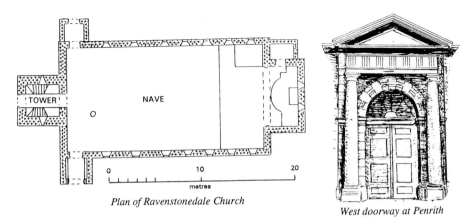

Plan of Ravenstonedale Church

West doorway at Penrith

PRESTON PATRICK   *St Gregory*   SD 546836

The church was built in 1852 to a design by Sharpe & Paley with a chancel added in 1892, but there is a 15th century window reset in the NW tower and on either side of the east window are two canopied niches which are also 15th century.

RAUGHTON HEAD   *No Dedication Known*   NY 379456

The church is of 1761 and has round-headed windows and a west tower with a neo-Norman top stage of 1881. The Venetian east window was altered in 1881.

RAVENSTONEDALE   *St Oswald*   NY 722043

The west tower is said to be of 1738 but the bell-openings look earlier. The wide main body of the church is of 1744 with seven lancets on each side. Towards the east end they are spaced more closely. The wide arch opening into the single bay chancel has 13th century responds. The porches look earlier than the church and that on the south has a reset outer entrance of c1200. The Georgian furnishings inside include a west gallery, a three-decker pulpit with a tester, box pews, a curved communion rail and the ten commandments held by painted figures of Moses and Aaron. Immediately to the north are the excavated lower parts of the east range of a Gilbertine priory with which the medieval church was connected.

RENWICK   *All Saints*   NY 597436

Only the two decker pulpit remains of the church built in 1733. The present church is of 1845 and contains a harmonium of about the same period.

ROCKCLIFFE   *St Mary*   NY 359617

In the churchyard is a fragment of a Saxon cross with a solid wheel-head, broad raised bands, interlace and dragons, and close to the west wall are a medieval graveslab and a Norman capital. The church is of 1848 to a design by James Stewart and the south porch-tower with a broach-spire is an addition of 1881.

RUSLAND   *St Paul*   SD 338897

Except for the west tower, the church erected in 1745 was mostly rebuilt in 1868.

St Bees Priory Church

Former south chapel arcade, St Bees

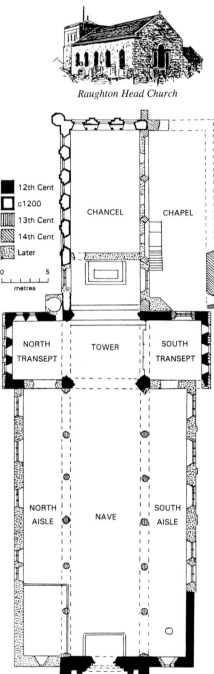

Raughton Head Church

Plan of St Bees Priory Church

ST BEES *St Mary & St Bega* NY 989121

A Benedictine nunnery was founded here c650. It was destroyed by the Danes but refounded by William de Meschines c1120. The cloister and its buildings have gone but the church remains fairly complete. Of the Norman period are the south transept with restored windows, the crossing with keeled demi-columns as responds, and the nave and south aisle west wall. The nave has a fine doorway of three orders with worn chevrons on the chamfered arches and capitals with figures, the columns now mostly being missing. In c1200 a fine new chancel was erected with long lancets shafted outside with waterleaf capitals. There are three lancets of equal height at the east end and internally these are separated by two tiers of tabernacles. Originally there was another shafted window above, but this was cut down when the present low-pitched roof was provided. The chancel now forms part of the school founded by Archbishop Grindal of York in 1583, the courtyard of which lies close to it. Only the blocked four bay arcade and the north jamb of the east window remain of a south chapel added in the early 14th century. The six bay nave arcades with alternating round and octagonal piers are 13th century, the capitals being decorated with small nailheads. One pier differs in having eight attached keeled shafts. The 15th century clerestory windows lie above the spandrels, not the arches. The nave west wall has three stepped lancets and canted buttresses built against smaller ones.

In the part used by the school is an effigy of Prior Cotyngham, d1300. An incised effigy of Joan de Lucy, d1369, lies in the north transept of c1200. There are many later monuments. Outside the church are two cross-shafts, one with interlace, the other with spirals and scrolls. An Early Norman lintel with a dragon and interlace lies over a gateway west of the church.

Scaleby Church

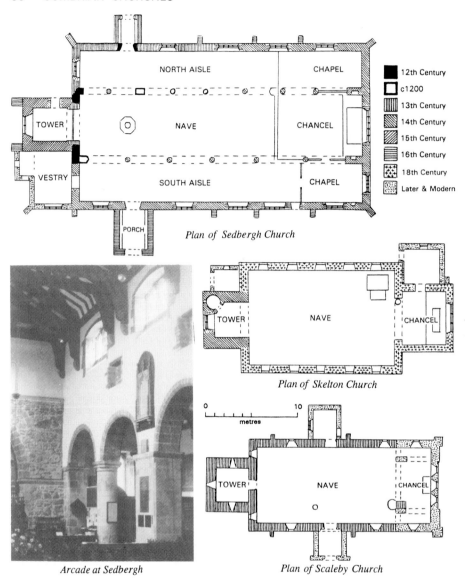

Plan of Sedbergh Church

	12th Century
	c1200
	13th Century
	14th Century
	15th Century
	16th Century
	18th Century
	Later & Modern

Plan of Skelton Church

Arcade at Sedbergh

Plan of Scaleby Church

SCALEBY   All Saints   NY 448632

As built c1200-20 the church comprised a west tower, a wide nave with clasping east buttresses, three lancets on each side, and round-headed doorways, plus a chancel which has now disappeared and its arch filled with three Victorian lancets. Also Victorian are the south porch, the north vestry and the piers inserted to create a chancel with narrow aisles in the nave east bay. The tower top is probably 17th century and the font is dated 1707. A sculptured fragment of c1200 has two sides showing figures of ecclesiastics, the other sides having once been attached.

SEDBERGH   *St Andrew*   SD 657921

There are traces of a Norman tower arch and a plain Norman north doorway. The SW respond is of c1200 but otherwise the six bay arcade goes with the 14th century south doorway. The north arcade is a real hotch-potch with two of the arches oddly stretched. Two bays west of a square pier are early 13th century, the next three bays are perhaps of c1200, and the three eastern bays are later. The north aisle west window and perhaps the tower with a corbelled-out bell-stage are 15th century. The clerestory, the east window with five stepped lancets under a segmental arch, and most of the other windows look early 16th century. The SW vestry is modern. The poor box is dated 1633 and the pulpit has an 18th century tester.

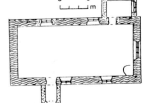

SETMURTHY   *St Barnabas*   NY 184322

The church is of 1794, but the features, including a polygonal SW baptistry and a polygonal NW turret, are of 1870. Inside is a font dated 1661 with initials and a simple geometrical pattern.

Plan of Soulby Chapel

SHAP   *St Michael*   NY 564154

The west tower is of 1828, the chancel is of 1898-9 and the rest seems mostly 19th century too. The four bay south arcade of c1200 has double-chamfered round arches on circular piers with round abaci.

SKELTON   *St Michael*   NY 439354

The west tower is 14th century. The wide nave of 1794 with thin round-arched windows is built on the bases of the outer walls of medieval aisles. One aisle contained a chantry of St Mary founded 1347. Of c1750 are the monument to Henry Richmond Brougham, the pulpit and the communion rail. The east window is of 1879.

SOULBY   *St Luke*   NY 749111

Sir Philip Musgrave built this single chamber in 1662-3. The round-headed south doorway with a late medieval type moulding and the bell turret betray the date.

Soulby Chapel

Sedbergh Church

STANWIX   *St Michael*   NY 401571

The church was rebuilt by John Hodgson in 1841 and an apse was added in 1893. There are three old grave slabs behind the organ and a Norman capital lies outside.

STRANDS   *No Dedication Known*   NY 124040

In 1830 a north aisle and vestry were added to a small chapel of uncertain date. The white coved ceiling is of the time of the Royal Arms used by George III from 1816 onwards. From York Minster have come the 17th century parts in the pulpit, lectern, and the panelling behind the altar.

STAVELEY   *St Margaret*   SD 472982

All that remains of the old church is a tower said to be of 1388. One window could be of that period. The bell-openings look 17th century and there are two tiny windows with moulded arches which could be older. The church of St James 1km NW is of 1864-5 by Crowther.

STAVELEY-IN-CARTMEL   *St Mary*   SD 379860

Walling may survive from a church recorded here in 1618, the period of one window with arched lights. The tower may be a relic of the rebuilding said to have taken place in 1793. Many features are of the restoration of 1897. The south arcade has timber piers.

Tower at Staveley

■ 12th Cent	〰 17th Cent
□ c1200	⊞ 18th Cent
▨ 14th Cent	▦ Later

0 ———————— 10 metres

NORTH
TRANSEPT

NORTH AISLE

NAVE

CHANCEL

SOUTH AISLE

Plan of Torpenhow Church

NORTH AISLE

NAVE

Plan of Strands Church

TOWER

Tower, Staveley

NAVE

TOWER

VESTRY

SOUTH AISLE

Plan of Staveley-in-Cartmel Church

Staveley-in-Cartmel Church

Torpenhow Church

TEMPLE SOWERBY *St James* NY 611271

The church of 1754 was given an aisle in 1770. The west tower is of 1807-8, the likely period of the lancet windows. The chancel and arcade are of 1873.

THRELKELD *St Mary* NY 322254

The main chamber is of 1777 with keyed-in round arched windows, a Venetian east window with a flat surround, and a broken pediment over the porch entrance. The oblong bell-turret with obelisks looks older. There is an organ of c1820. See p11.

THURSBY *St Andrew* NY 324504

The church is of 1846 with window tracery of 1878 but some of the tablets to the Brisco family of Crofton Hall go back to the mid 18th century.

TORPENHOW *St Michael* NY 205398

Norman are the north aisle doorway, the chancel north windows and traces of others in the south wall. A window with intersecting tracery of c1300 has replaced two more in the east wall. The north transept is also of c1300. Of c1170 are the arcades of three bays with single step arches and the doorway in the south aisle with chevrons and a rope on the arch, a reel motif on the hood-mould and triple responds with figures on the capitals and chevrons on the abaci. The upper parts of the south aisle with battlements, and probably also the bellcote, are 17th century. The nave has a painted ceiling with cupids and garlands said to have come from the hall of a London livery company, being given to the church in 1689. The Norman font has intersecting arches and loose knots and interlacing. There is a plain Jacobean pulpit.

TROUTBECK *Jesus Chapel* NY 413028

The west tower is of 1736. The nave and chancel may be of 1828 or of 1879. Jacobean woodwork from Calgarth Hall has been used to make the stalls and communion rail. There are two collecting shovels dated 1692.

ULDALE   *St James*   NY 240380

The whitewashed nave is mostly of c1730 but Norman work survives in the north and west walls. The chancel arch is 16th century but the chancel was rebuilt in 1837 when a vestry was added. There is a worn graveslab with a chalice. St Mary's, a chapel of ease mentioned in 1310, decayed by 1518, was sold in the 1550s.

ULPHA   *St John*   NY 198933

This is a low dale chapel with domestic looking windows of late date except for the east window which may be 17th century. Wall waintings of the 17th and 18th centuries including Royal Arms of Queen Anne were revealed in 1934. See p10.

ULVERSTON   *St Mary*   SD 289787

The Norman south doorway with incised chevrons has obviously been moved and reassambled at some time. The arcades are 15th or early 16th century. The west tower was built shortly after an older tower collapsed in a gale in 1540, and the clerestory and the low-pitched roof with alternating hammer-beams and tiebeams are probably of the same period. The outer walls of the wide aisles are of the restoration of 1864-6 by Austin & Paley, and the chancel was lengthened in 1904. There is no chancel arch. On a tomb chest are recumbent effigies of William Sandys, d1559, and his wife. There are brasses of Myles Dodding, d1606, and his wife within a stone surround. Another Myles Dodding, d1629, has a tablet with a recumbent effigy between columns. There is a cartouche signed by Christopher Mason to John Braddyll of Conishead Priory, d1727, and there is a small bust to Thomas Braddyll, d1776.

On chapel island 6km to the SE is a ruined chapel with three lancet windows in the east gable. Other parts were built in 1823 to make the ruin into a folly.

Ulverston Church

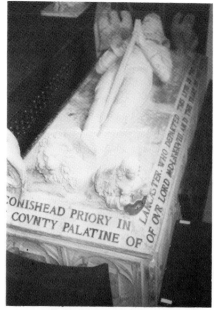
Tomb in Ulverston Church

Urswick Church

URSWICK   *St Mary*   SD 268742

The chancel was lengthened in the 14th century and has windows of that period. The east window of 1908 is said to reproduce what was there before. The wide west tower is mostly late medieval and has upon it a contemporary sculpture of the Pieta, but the lowest stage may be 13th century. The church contains part of an 11th century Anglo-Saxon cross-shaft with interlace, a runic inscription and two men either side of a cross. A 13th century foliated coffin lid has an inscription referring to Amicitia, daughter of John Francis. There are several 18th and 19th century tablets, a three decker pulpit, a Georgian west Galley on pairs of Tuscan Columns, an 18th century altar painting by James Cranke, and much fine woodwork of 1909-12.

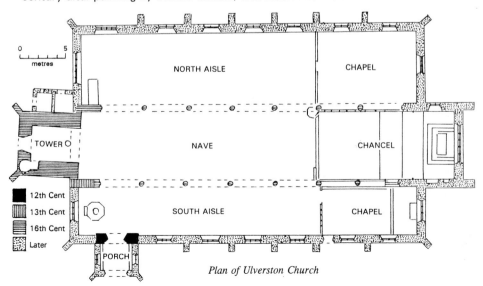

Plan of Ulverston Church

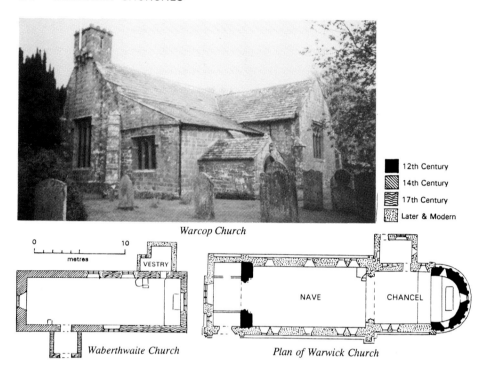

■	12th Century
▨	14th Century
▤	17th Century
▦	Later & Modern

Warcop Church

Waberthwaite Church

Plan of Warwick Church

WABERTHWAITE   *St John Evangelist*   SD 100951

This is a low single chamber beside the Esk estuary. The west window is 15th century. The other windows with pairs of arched lights are 16th or 17th century when the building was probably lengthened to the east. Inside are box pews, a pulpit dated 1630 and a font formed of a black block with broaches at the corners. In the churchyard is a fragment of a cross-shaft with interlace with figures and an animal. In the vestry lie fragments of a second cross-shaft.

Warwick Church

WARCOP   *St Columba*   NY 743157

The nave is Norman and the boiler-house conceals evidence of an original doorway. In the 13th century the church was given transepts with piscinas and a new chancel, although the latter was rebuilt in 1855 except for the chancel arch. The north transept has restored lancets. The south transept has original clasping corner buttresses but the east and south windows are 14th century, the period of the defaced female effigy. In the 15th century the nave was given a new west wall with bold diagonal buttresses and a south aisle was added with a two bay arcade. The porch is 17th century. In the churchyard are re-erected medieval fragments of a 13th century window and a late medieval doorway from Burton Hall, demolished in 1957.

WARWICK   *St Leonard*   NY 466568

Most of the church is of c1870 by R.J.Withers but there is a fine Norman arch of 1130 below the bellcote at the west end and on a chancel buttress is a rebus of Prior Thornton of Wetheral i.e. early 16th century. The east end is a genuine Norman apse with three small windows and closely spaced pilaster strips carrying arches. Nothing quite like this remains elsewhere in Britain but it has been suggested that it was copied from the design of the original Norman east end of Carlisle Cathedral.

WASDALE   *No Dedication Known*   NY 188088

This is a small single chamber with mullioned windows of uncertain date. There is just 1.9m of headroom under the tie-beams. The oil lamp brackets are Victorian.

WESTWARD   *St Hilda*

NY 274459

The church seems to be of the same period as the school of 1828 but it contains a brass to Richard Barnise, d1648 and another recording a legacy of Francis Barnise.

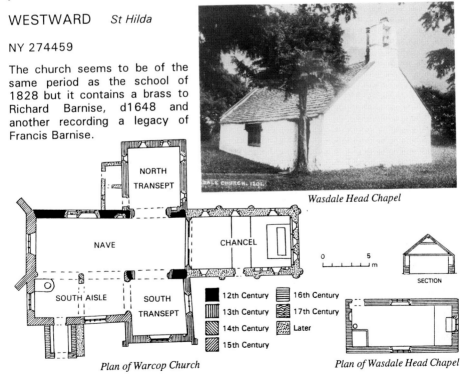

Wasdale Head Chapel

Plan legend:
- ■ 12th Century
- ▥ 13th Century
- ▧ 14th Century
- ▨ 15th Century
- ▤ 16th Century
- ▩ 17th Century
- ▦ Later

Plan of Warcop Church   *Plan of Wasdale Head Chapel*

WETHERAL   *Holy Trinity*   NY 467544

The exterior is mostly early 16th century with two and three light windows with round-arched lights and the chancel has inscriptions relating to William Thornton and Richard de Wetheral, the last two priors of the Benedictine priory founded c1100 by Ranulph de Meschines, which lay just to the south of the church. The west tower is of about the time when the Howards of Corby Castle added a five bay mausoleum to house the monument of Lady Maria, d1789, but the tower upper stage is of 1882. The chancel was mostly rebuilt in 1872. The much restored arcades of four bays with double-chamfered arches on circular piers are 13th century. In the west window are stained glass saints and kneeling donors of the 15th century. On a tomb chest of c1500 with shields in quatrefoils at the north aisle east end are two defaced effigies of Sir Richard Salkeld, d1500 and his wife Jane Vaux. See page 6.

WHICHAM   *St Mary*   SD 119840

The wide single chamber has a south doorway with a chamfered round arch which is Norman. The east window is 17th century. The north transept was added in 1857 and the windows were then restored.

WHITBECK   *St Mary*   SD 134827

The church was much restored in 1883. A 13th century arch divides off the east end the same width as the rest and there is a defaced 14th century female effigy.

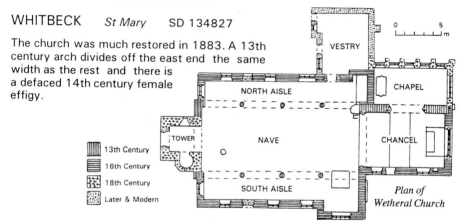

0   5 m

VESTRY

NORTH AISLE

CHAPEL

TOWER

NAVE

CHANCEL

|||| 13th Century

≡ 16th Century

▦ 18th Century

▨ Later & Modern

O

SOUTH AISLE

Plan of Wetheral Church

Wetheral Church

St James' Church, Whitehaven

WHITEHAVEN   *St James*   NX 976185

This church of 1752-3 has a broad tower with obelisk pinnacles which faces down Queen Street, hence the show front with an extra pediment above that of the doorway. The aisles embrace the tower and have two tiers of windows. The interior is the finest of its period in Cumbria and has galleries reached by a staircase in the tower. Tuscan columns support the galleries and Ionic columns rise to the flat ceiling with stucco roundels painted with scenes of the Ascension and angels and the Vigin with angels. There is an apse with Ionic pilasters. Contemporary with the church are the communion rail of Roman Ionic balusters, and the lofty pulpit with fluted pilasters and arched panels. Of the same period is the fine altarpiece by Guilio Cesare Procaccini depicting the Transfiguration and donated by the 3rd Earl of Lonsdale.

WHITEHAVEN   *St Nicholas*   NX 974182

Of the church of 1693, which was a long building with windows in two tiers, there remains only the west doorway inside the west porch of the church of 1883 designed by C.J.Ferguson for Margaret Gibson as a memorial to her parents. The church of Holy Trinity built in 1715 at the east end of Roper Street has been destroyed, and the third church of the town is now Christ Church of 1847 by Waller in Preston Street.

Wigton Church

WIGTON *St Mary* NY 256484

This church of 1788 designed by the masons Nixson and Parkin is very similar to that of St Cuthbert at Carlisle. The nave of eight bays has two tiers of windows in the middle bays and doorways at either end. These doorways and that in the tower have rusticated quoins. Galleries upon Tuscan columns are reached by stairs in lobbies flanking the tower. The flat ceiling has stucco ornamentation in two roundels and an oval. The short chancel has a Venetian window with fluted Ionic columns. The pulpit is contemporary. The retable of the altar in the north aisle has German 16th and 17th century woodwork. In the churchyard to the south is a late 13th century window remaining from the old church. It has a sexfoiled circle over two cusped lights.

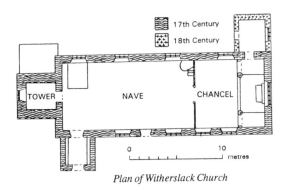

17th Century
18th Century

TOWER NAVE CHANCEL

0   10   metres

Plan of Witherslack Church

Window of Old Church, Wigton

WITHERSLACK   *St Paul*   NY 432842

This plain Gothic church was built c1669 under the terms of the will of John Barwick, Dean of St Pauls, and his brother, Charles II's physician, both born in this parish. It conprises a wide single chamber, a west tower and south porch. In 1768 the church was heightened and the windows were then continued further up and given transoms where their heads once were. They are of three lights with arched heads. The east window is of five stepped lights under a segmental arch. A second south doorway has an inscription in a cartouche. The coved ceiling and the screen of Ionic columns dividing off the sanctuary are of 1768. The lectern has panels of c1670 and there is heraldic glass of that period. The pulpit has parts of the original three decker pulpit of c1670. The tester is of c1768. There are Royal Arms of Queen Anne dated 1710.

Witherslack Church

Wythburn Church

WORKINGTON   *St Michael*   NX 997290

The church lies slightly away from the town centre. It is of 1770 with an upper tier of windows for lighting galleries but was remodelled in 1887-90 after a fire and is now ruined after another fire in 1994. The tower remains in use for services and under it are three cross-slabs with swords, a scalloped Norman capital and four fragments of Anglo-Danish cross-shafts. The church also has a Norman arch inside with a roll and hollow and a late medieval font. The early 15th century tomb chest with effigies of a knight and lady was badly damaged in the 1994 fire and has been removed for repair. She has two angels by her pillow and two puppies biting her skirt.

WYTHBURN   *No Dedication Known*   NY 324136

This church with square side windows set beside Thirlmere was built in 1640. It was given an apse and south vestry in 1872.

WYTHOP   *St Margaret*   NY 194291

A ruined chapel lacking features but probably of 16th or 17th century date lies by a track east of Kelsick Farm 1km SE of the church of 1865-6 by Bruce.

Plan of Wythburn Church

Wythop Chapel

ALLONBY - Christ Church - 1845, in Georgian style. On site of church of 1744.
ALSTON - St Augustine - 1870 by J.W.Walton. Contains slightly earlier monuments.
AMBLESIDE - St Anne - 1812, on Chapel Hill. Now de-consecrated.
AMBLESIDE - St Mary - 1850-4 by Sir G.G.Scott. Large church with SE tower.
ARLECDON - St Michael - 1829, remodelled and tower added 1904.
ARNSIDE - St James - 1866 by Miles Thompson. Enlarged 1905 and 1914.
BARBON - St Bartholomew - 1893 by Paley & Austin. Crossing tower with turret.
BARDSEA - Holy Trinity - 1843-53 by George Webster. Tower with spire, and apse.
BARROW-IN-FURNESS - St George - 1859-61 by E.G.Paley, north aisle added 1867.
BARROW-IN-FURNESS - St James - 1867-9 by E.G.Paley. Brick with a spire and apse.
BARROW-IN-FURNESS - St John - 1935 by Seely & Paget. Cruciform, & of concrete.
BARROW-IN-FURNESS - St Luke - 1962 by Cruickshank & Seward. Detached tower.
BARROW-IN-FURNESS - St Matthew - 1965-7 by Schomberg Scott.
BARROW-IN-FURNESS - St Paul - 1871 by Habershon & Brock. Post-war extensions.
BLACKFORD - St John Baptist - 1870 by Borough. Nave, chancel & spired bellcote.
BORROWDALE - Early 19th century nave, chancel 1873. Whitewashed dale chapel.
BRATHAY - Holy Trinity - 1836 for Giles Redmayne of Brathay Hall.
BROUGHTON EAST - 1892-4 by Paley, Austin & Paley. Cruciform, high central tower.
BROUGHTON MOOR - St Columba - 1905 by Caroe. Rock-faced, north porch-tower.
BURNESIDE - St Oswald - 1880-1 by Ferguson. Large, Dec style, SW tower.
BUTTERMERE - 1841 - Small nave & chancel with bellcote in a lovely position.
CALDER BRIDGE - St Bridget - 1842 by E.Sharpe. Cruciform with a west tower.
CALTHWAITE - 1913, probably by Unwin. Gothic, with lancets. Interesting pulpit.
CARLISLE - Holy Trinity - 1828-30 by Rickman & Hutchinson.
CARLISLE - St Aidan - 1899-1902 by C.J.Ferguson. Large, in Decorated style.
CARLISLE - St James - 1865-7 by Andrews & Pepper. Large, with apse & SW tower.
CARLISLE - St John Evangelist - 1867 by R.Clarke. In London Rad.
CARLISLE - St Paul - 1868-75 by Habershon & Brock. Geometrical tracery.
CASTERTON - Holy Trinity - School chapel 1831-3, chancel added c1860.
CASTLE CARROCK - 1828, remodelled inside in 1888. Thin west tower.
CASTLERIGG - St John - 1845, tower & single low chamber, restored in 1893.
CAUTLEY - St Mark - 1847 by Butterfield. Small, of little interest.
CLEATOR MOOR - St John Evangelist - 1870-2 by George Ferguson. Neo-Norman.
COCKERMOUTH - All Saints - 1852-4 by Joseph Clarke, replacing a church of 1711.
COCKERMOUTH - Christ Church - 1865 by Bruce. Plate tracery. Pinnacled tower.
CONISTON - St Andrew - 1819 by Matson, chancel 1891. Replaced chapel of 1586.
COTEHILL - St John Evangelist - 1868 by Habershon & Brock. Geometrical. NE tower.
COWGILL - St John Evangelist - 1838, small and plain.
CROGLIN - St John Baptist - 1878 by J Howison. Defaced female effigy lies outside.
CROSBY-ON-EDEN - St John Evangelist - 1854 by R.H.Billings.
CROSSCRAKE - St Thomas - 1875 by Paley & Austin. Nave, chancel and transepts.
CROSTHWAITE - St Mary - 1878. Rockfaced with west tower and shallow east apse.
CUMDIVOCK - St John Evangelist - 1871 by Cory & Ferguson.
DALTON-IN-FURNESS - St Margaret - 1902-4 by Preston.
DRIGG - St Peter - 1850. Single chamber with lancets and a north aisle.
EAGLESFIELD - 1891 by C.F.Ferguson. Nave and chancel. Square-headed windows.
EGTON - St Mary - 1856 by Thompson, altered 1864. On site of church of c1780.
EMBLETON - St Cuthbert - 1806 with thin west tower. Remodelled in 1884.
FARLAM - St Thomas Becket - 1860 by Salvin. Nave, north aisle, chancel, bellcote.
FAR SAWREY - St Peter - 1866-72 by Robert Brass. Cruciform with NE tower.
FINSTHWAITE - St Peter - 1873-4 by Paley & Austin. Replaced church of 1724.
FIRBANK - St John Evangelist - 1842 by Bateman. Nave with lancets, short chancel.

FLIMBY - St Nicholas - 1794, but entirely remodelled in 1862.
FLOOKBURGH - St John - 1897-1900 by Austin & Paley. Contains regalia of c1600.
FRIZINGTON - St Paul - 1867-8. Wide, hammerbeam roof, and lancets. SW turret.
GAMBLESBY - St John - 1866 by C.J.Ferguson. Single chamber with apse.
GARRIGILL - St John - 1790, single chamber entirely remodelled in the 1890s.
GATESGILL - 1869 - Nave & chancel with asymmetrically placed bellcote.
GILSLAND - St Mary Magdalene - 1852-4 by James Stewart. Single & paired lancets.
GRANE-IN-BORROWDALE - 1860. Single chamber with round-arched windows.
GRANGE-OVER-SANDS - St Paul - 1853-4 by Murray, aisles 1861-7, chancel 1932.
GRAYRIGG - St John - 1837. Lancets and a flat ceiling. West tower added 1869.
GREAT ASBY - St Peter - 1866 by Hay & Hay. Geometrical tracery. Fine south porch.
GREAT LANGDALE - Holy Trinity - 1857 by John Cory. At Chapel Stile. South tower.
HAVERTHWAITE - St Anne - 1824-5. Nave, chancel and west tower. Y-tracery.
HAYTON - St James - 1868 by Travers. Nave, bellcote and chancel beside a green.
HENSINGHAM - St John Evengelist - 1911-13 by J.Slack. Rockfaced with NE tower.
HETHERSGILL - St Mary - 1876 by Brock. Rockfaced, nave with bellcote and chancel.
HOLME LOW - St Paul - 1845 by William Armstrong. Nave with bellcote and chancel.
HOUGHTON - St John Evangelist - 1840. West tower with Y-tracery, nave, chancel.
HOWGILL - Holy Trinity - 1838 by Edmund Sharpe. Lancets.
HUTTON ROOF - St John - 1881-2 by Paley & Austin. South porch-tower, north aisle.
IRELETH - St Mary - 1865, replacing Episcopal chapel of 1612. Small north tower.
IVEGILL - Christ Church - 1868 by R.J.Withers & Putney. Polygonal bell-turret.
KENDAL - St George - 1839-41 by G.Webster. Chancel 1910-11 by Austin & Paley.
KENDAL - St Thomas - 1837 by G.Webster. Lancets with engaged west tower.
KESWICK - St John Evangelist - 1838 by Salvin, aisles added 1862 and 1882.
LEVENS - St John Evangelist - 1828. Nave and chancel. Octagonal spired bell turret.
LINDALE - St Paul - 1828 with west tower. Later chancel, north aisle added 1912.
LITTLE BROUGHTON - Christ Church - 1858. Nave, bellcote, & chancel with lancets.
LITTLE STRICKLAND - St Mary - 1814. Windows with Y-tracery.
LONG SLEDDALE - 1863. Nave and chancel with small lancets and bellcote.
LORTON - St Cuthbert - Early 19th century. Embraced west tower, small lancets.
LOWESWATER - St Bartholomew - 1827, but most features of 1884 remodelling.
LOWICK - St Luke - 1885. West tower and single chamber with lancets.
MANSERGH - 1880 by Paley & Austin. Contains a Georgian baluster font.
MARDALE - Holy Trinity - Submerged by the waters of Haweswater Reservoir.
MARTINDALE - St Peter - 1880-2 by J.A.Cory. Nave and chancel, lancet windows.
MARYPORT - Christchurch - 1872 by Eaglesfield. Apse and NE tower.
MIDDLETON - Holy Ghost - 1878-9 by C.J.Ferguson. Nave, chancel and bellcote.
MILNTHORPE - St Thomas - 1837, tower and paired lancets. Chancel added 1883.
MURTON - St John - 1856 by G.Robinson. Three decker pulpit middle of N side.
NATLAND - St Mark - 1909-10 by Paley & Austin. Aisled with big west tower.
NENTHEAD - St John - 1845 with polygonal bell-turret. Much altered in 1907.
NEW HUTTON - St Stephen - 1828-8 by George Webster. Lancets, west tower.
NEWLANDS - 1843, single chamber with round arched windows. Restored 1885.
NICHOLFOREST - St Nicholas - 1866-7 by Alexander Graham. Rockfaced with apse.
OSMOTHERLEY - St John Evangelist - 1874 by Paley & Austin. Apse, spired bellcote.
PATTERDALE - St Patrick - 1853 by Salvin. Small. Saddleback roofed NE tower.
PENRUDDOCK - All Saints - 1902 by C.J.Ferguson. Roughcast single chamber.
PLUMPTON WALL - St John Evangelist - 1907 by Sir Robert Lorimer.
POOLEY BRIDGE - St Paul - 1868 by Cory & Ferguson. Bell-turret with spire.
RAMPSIDE - St Michael - 1840, chancel 1892. Replaced chapel of 1621.
ROSLEY - Holy Trinity - 1840. Single chancel with lancets. Thin west tower.

RYDAL - St Mary - 1824. West tower and nave and chancel with tracery of 1884.
SATTERTHWAITE - Of uncertain date with a SW porch. Early 18th century plate.
SCOTBY - 1854 by Salvin. Nave and chancel with tower on south side.
SEASCALE - St Cuthbert - 1890 by C.J.Ferguson. Nave, south aisle, chancel.
SEATHWAITE - Holy Trinity - 1874 for H.W.Schneider. Replaced older chapel.
SEATON - St Paul - 1883 by George Watson. Thin NE tower and polygonal apse.
SEBERGHAM - St Mary - 1825, remodelled 1905. Nave and chancel, thin west tower.
SELSIDE - St Thomas - 1838 with a tower of 1894. Contains an 18th century font.
SILLOTH - Christ Church - 1870-1 by Cory & Ferguson. Big, apse, NW porch-tower.
SKELSMERGH - St John Baptist - 1871 by Joseph Birtley. Nave and chancel.
SKIRWITH - St John Evangelist - 1856 by Francis & Francis. SW tower & spire.
STAPLETON - St Mary - 1830. West tower, wide nave, chancel. Sited alone.
TALKIN - 1842. Neo-Norman nave and chancel with fittings in same style.
TEBAY - St James - 1880 by C.J.Ferguson. Rockfaced with apsidal west baptistry.
THWAITES - St Anne - 1854 by E.G.Paley. Plate tracery in nave, lancets in chancel.
THORNTHYWAITE - St Mary - Cruciform, details 1831, 1853. Walls perhaps c1760.
TORVER - St Luke - 1884 by Paley & Austin. Buttressed central tower.
ULVERSTON - Holy Trinity - 1829-32 by Anthony Salvin. NW tower with spire.
UNDERBARROW - All Saints - 1869. Polygonal apse and spired south porch-turret.
UPPERBY - St John - 1840, lancets and west tower with Y-tracery.
WALNEY ISLAND - St Mary - 1907-8 by Austin & Paley.
WALTON - St Mary - 1869-70 by Paley. Nave, north aisle, NW tower.
WARWICK BRIDGE - St Paul - 1845 by Dobson. Neo-Norman, apse. Broach-spire.
WATERMILLOCK - All Saints - 1884 by C.J.Ferguson. Wide tower, nave, chancel.
WAVERTON - Christ Church - 1865. Nave with bellcote & plate tracery. Chancel.
WEST NEWTON - St Matthew - 1857 by Hugall. Geometrical tracery. Nave, chancel.
WINDERMERE - St Mary - 1848, aisles 1850s, transept 1871, tower & chancel 1881.
WINDERMERE - St John Evangelist - 1886 by Joseph Pattinson. Cruciform.
WINSTER - Holy Trinity - 1875, single chamber with bellcote on a mid-buttress.
WOODLAND - 1891 by J.W.Grundy & Sons. Nave with bellcote and apse.
WORKINGTON - St John - 1823 by Thomas Hardwick. Tower 1846, Tuscan portico.
WRAY - St Margaret - 1845 for James Dawson of Wray Castle.
WREAY - St Mary - c1840, Roman basilica with apse designed by patron Sara Losh.
Note: Orientations given in this section are sometimes ritual rather than actual.

FURTHER READING

The Buildings of Cumberland and Westmorland, Nikolaus Pevsner, 1967.
The Buildings of North Lancashire, Nicholaus Pevsner, 1969
The Medieval Fortified Buildings of Cumbria, Denis R Perriam & John Robinson, 1998.
Transactions of Cumberland and Westmorland Antiquarian and Archeological Society.
Royal Commission on Historical Monuments inventory for Westmorland, 1936.
Victorian County Histories for Cumberland, Lancashire and Yorkshire (several vols).
History of Cumberland, W.Hutchinson, 2 vols, 1794, reprinted 1974.
Guide pamphlets are or have been available at various parish churches such as:
    Abbeytown (Hulme Cultram) Bolton, Bromfield, Burgh-by-Sands, Cartmel,
    Crosthwaite, Gosforth, Grasmere, Hawkshead, Lanercost, Long Marton, Penrith

GLOSSARY OF ARCHITECTURAL TERMS

Abacus	- A flat slab on top of a capital.
Apse	- Semi-circular or polygonal east end of a church containing an altar.
Ashlar	- Masonry of blocks with even faces and square edges.
Ballflower	- Globular flower of three petals enclosing a ball. Curent c1310-40.
Baroque	- A whimsical and odd form of the Classical architectural style.
Beakhead	- Decorative motif of bird or beast heads, often biting a roll moulding.
Broaches	- Sloping half pyramids adapting an octagonal spire to a square tower.
Cartouche	- A tablet with an ornate frame, usually enclosing an inscription.
Chancel	- The eastern part of a church used by the clergy.
Chevron Ornament	- A Norman ornament with continuous Vs forming a zig-zag.
Clerestory	- An upper storey pierced by windows lighting the floor below.
Collar Beam	- A tie-beam used higher up near the apex of the roof.
Corbel Table	- A row of corbels supporting the eaves of a roof.
Crossing Tower	- A tower built on four arches in the middle of a cruciform church.
Cruciform Church	- A cross-shaped church with transepts forming the arms of the cross.
Cusp	- A projecting point between the foils of a foiled Gothic arch.
Dado	- The decorative covering of the lower part of a wall or screen.
Decorated	- The architecture style in vogue in England c1300-1380.
Dog Tooth	- Four centered stars placed diagonally and raised pyramidally.
Easter Sepulchre	- A recess in a chancel which received an effigy of Christ at Easter.
Elizabethan	- Of the time of Queen Elizabeth I (1558-1603).
Fan Vault	- Vault with fan-like patterns. In fashion from c1440 to 1530.
Foil	- A lobe formed by the cusping of a circle or arch.
Four Centred Arch	- A low, flattish arch with each curve drawn from two compass points.
Head Stops	- Heads of humans or beasts forming the ends of a hoodmould.
Hoodmould	- A projecting moulding above a lintel or arch to throw off water.
Jacobean	- Of the time of King James I (1603-25).
Jamb	- The side of a doorway, window, or other opening.
King-post	- An upright timber connecting a tie-beam with a collar-beam.
Lancet	- A long and comparatively narrow window with a pointed head.
Light	- A compartment of a window.
Lintel	- A horizontal stone or beam spanning an opening.
Miserichord	- Bracket underneath hinged choir stall seat to support standing person.
Mullion	- A vertical member dividing the lights of a window.
Nave	- The part of a church in which the congregation sits or stands.
Nook-Shaft	- A shaft set in the angle of a pier or respond or jamb of a window.
Norman	- A division of English Romanesque architecture from 1066 to 1200.
Ogival Arch	- Arch of oriental origin with both convex and concave curves.
Pediment	- Low-pitch gable used in classical and neo-classical architecture.
Perpendicular	- The architectural style in vogue in England c1380-1540.
Pilaster	- Flat buttress or pier attached to a wall.
Piscina	- A stone basin used for rinsing out holy vessels after a mass.
Plinth	- The projecting base of a wall.
Quoins	- Dressed stones at the corners of a building.
Rere-Arch	- An arch on the inside face of a window embrasure or doorway.
Reredos	- Structure behind and above an altar forming a backdrop to it.
Respond	- A half pier or column bonded into a wall and carrying an arch.
Reticulation	- Tracery with a net-like appearence. Current c1330-70.
Rood Screen	- A screen with a crucifix mounted on it between a nave and chancel.
Sedilia	- Seats for clergy (usually three) in the south wall of a chancel.
Tester	- A sounding board above a 17th or 18th century pulpit.
Tie-Beam	- A beam connecting the slopes of a roof at or near its foot.
Tracery	- Intersecting ribwork in the upper part of a later Gothic window.
Transom	- A horizontal member dividing the lights of a window.
Triptych	- Three surfaces, usually sculpted or painted, joined by hinges.
Tympanum	- The space between the lintel of a doorway and the arch above it.
Venetian Window	- Window with square headed light on either side of an arched light.
Victorian	- Of the time of Queen Victoria (1837-1901).
Wind Braces	- Struts use to strengthen the sloping sides of a gabled roof.